Belief in a Mixed Society

D0240868

Western society is now irretrievably mixed and pluralist. In Bradford a third of babies born are of Asian origin. 30 schools in the inner city have more than 50 per cent Asian Muslim children. A councillor told a BBC Panorama team: 'We're sitting on a time-bomb here. You've only got to look at the figures to see what the risks are.'

What happens to religious conviction in such a society? Many from Muslim and Hindu backgrounds see the West as bankrupt of moral and spiritual values. Those from a traditional Christian background may be deeply suspicious of the 'threat' of non-Christian cultures.

How far are schools a battleground, how far are they a unifying influence in society? What is the place of religion in schools? How far should we respect different attitudes to women in society, to marriage and the family? Food, health, morality and the law, attitudes to work, to freedom and truth in the media, to wealth and power, all these are areas in which people have to come to terms with those of other faiths or none.

This important book is by Christian theologian Christopher Lamb, who writes from experience of living in an Asian culture, academic study of Islam and from constant contact with the most pluralist parts of Britain. From 1979 he has been co-ordinator of the Other Faiths Theological Project, run jointly by two Anglican missionary societies. He and his family live in Birmingham, where his wife teaches English to children newly-arrived in the country.

For such value as this book may have I am indebted to innumerable friends, colleagues and teachers, but above all to the loving forbearance and glorious sanity of my wife Tina. It is dedicated in gratitude to God for our eldest daughter Ruth, who died in Pakistan, aged eight.

'And a little child shall lead them.'

Belief in a
Mixed Society

CHRISTOPHER LAMB

A LION PAPERBACK
Tring · Belleville · Sydney

Copyright © 1985 Christopher Lamb

Published by
Lion Publishing plc
Icknield Way, Tring, Herts, England
ISBN 0 85648 210 2
Lion Publishing Corporation
10885 Textile Road, Belleville, Michigan 48111, USA
ISBN 0 85648 210 2
Albatross Books
PO Box 320, Sutherland, NSW 2232, Australia
ISBN 0 86760 577 4

First edition 1985

Quotations from the Bible are taken from the following versions:
The New English Bible, second edition, copyright 1970 Oxford and Cambridge
University Presses.
Good News Bible, copyright 1966. 1971 and 1976 American Bible Society, published
by Bible Societies/Collins.
Authorized King James Version of the Bible, Crown copyright.
Revised Standard Version of the Bible, copyright 1946 and 1952, second edition 1971,
Division of Christian Education, National Council of the Churches of Christ in the
USA.
The Jerusalem Bible, copyright 1966, 1967 and 1968 Darton, Longman and Todd
Ltd and Doubleday and Company Inc.

British Library Cataloguing in Publication Data

Lamb, C.A.
    Belief in a mixed society.
    1. Christianity and other religions   2. Great
    Britain——Religion
    I. Title
    291'.0941   BR127
    ISBN 0-85648-210-2

Printed and bound in Great Britain by
Cox and Wyman, Reading

Contents

Introduction

My wife, in company with our dog, was handed a petition on the station of an English county town. The lady presenting it said to this evident animal-lover 'Do you know about ritual slaughter?' My wife replied, Yes, she did, a little (enough to be going on with, anyway). The petition turned out to be aimed at preventing local Muslims from establishing their own slaughter-house in a nearby town, on the grounds that the Muslim ritual method of slaughter was cruel to animals. My wife, now fully engaged in the conversation, explained that we had been missionaries in Pakistan, and thought that people had to be free to follow their convictions on this kind of issue. If Muslim law prescribed certain details on the consumption and preparation of food, as it did, Muslim citizens of Britain should be able to observe them, as Jews observed their laws.

The lady was taken aback by this unexpected opposition, and retreated from uncomfortable ground to broader principles. 'Well,' she said, 'we didn't ask them to come here, but since they are here they ought to accept our way of doing things. Why should we have to accept theirs?' My wife murmured something about racial equality and the acceptance of other cultures, but the petition was now forgotten and history surveyed from a higher vantage-point. 'After all,' said the lady triumphantly, 'what did we fight the last war for?'

In Britain some find this line of argument persuasive, however unconvincing it may be to more liberal ears. The image of Dunkirk, the little ships rescuing the straggling survivors of a beaten army to fight again, expresses for many people the fragility of an island constantly threatened, yet unstained by alien influence, undefeated by the dark tides which again and again have threatened her shores. Today the Germans are allies, and so cannot be the danger now facing us. Yet 'the last war' is still unwon, for the enemy has now revealed himself as a more remotely alien power, a non-

European threat to the fundamental values and inherited culture of the British people. And since this supposed danger is accompanied by economic recession and unmistakable decline from greatness as a world power, the new cultural forces are felt more than ever to be invading forces of darkness, to represent a return to savagery.

The lady claimed that the churches supported her petition. Whether they did or not, others within the churches see Britain as a haven of enlightenment. A Bradford lady went to her Mothers' Union meeting to listen to the Indian wife of the curate speaking about her native country. During the questions she got to her feet: 'Do you think there will come a time when your people are civilized, like us?' The compatriot of Gandhi and the Buddha paused before she replied, 'Yes –and I dread it.' Neither Bradford schools nor the Mothers' Union are responsible for the kind of literature which must have formed that lady's basic outlook (though both may be charged with failing to remove its effects).

My mother, recounting someone's inexplicable behaviour, would invariably conclude her tale with the words 'Can't understand it. Nor could any other white man.' It was years before I registered the unconscious racism of that remark. The unwelcome fact is that in the West as a whole a sense of white superiority has pervaded much of the literature of children's stories and school history and geography textbooks. It is only comparatively recently that Third World authors themselves have thrown off this crippling assumption, and begun to question not only the alleged superiority of the white man's culture but even the desirability of 'modernization' as a process to be adopted, or at least hoped for in their own countries. As many see it, mounting unemployment, street riots and the disintegration of traditional family life place large question marks over Western claims to be a 'civilized' or 'civilizing' force in the world.

Western society is now irretrievably mixed, pluralist in character. This has happened partly because of the break-down of a single world-view, a process beginning many centuries ago. Partly it is a visible and obvious fact to be seen in every major city, where Caucasian and Afro-Caribbean, South Asian and Chinese ethnic types jostle on every street.

The questions of the 1981 British census were available in English, Welsh, Bengali, Cantonese, Greek, Gujarati, Hindi, Italian, Punjabi, Turkish and Urdu, but few would feel that a country of Britain's size should aim to match polyglot India, with its 600 million people and fourteen official languages. There must be basic agreement on the laws by which we are governed. Should the demand of some Muslims be accepted that Islamic family law be enforced on Muslims in Britain? It cannot be claimed that the demand is impossible to meet, since British officials operated a communal law system for generations in the days of empire. If the demand is rejected it can only be because of a clear understanding of the cultural and ideological basis of British society. Similarly there must be basic agreement on the political forms by which our laws and the day to day economic and social circumstances of our lives are regulated.

What happens to religious conviction in such a society? When different ways of life are followed in the same city, and within the same national framework, how do people decide what adjustments to make to their own ways, and what will they insist upon as essential for the satisfactory life of the whole community? How, in fact, is 'the community' to be defined? In the accelerating changes brought about by technology, the pressures and problems of pluralism are vastly accentuated by the presence, as fellow-citizens in Britain but in some countries as migrant workers, of hundreds of thousands who do not share even the post-Christian framework of the majority but whose assumptions and attitudes and way of life are shaped by Islam, Hinduism, Sikhism or varieties of Buddhism and Chinese religion. Each person has to come to terms with the presence of these others, and to decide how far their ways of thinking should be allowed to shape his or her life.

For myself, as a Christian, I see great testing and therefore great value for Christian understanding in the painful sifting process brought about by religious and cultural pluralism. For too long religion has been identified in the European mind with Christianity. For too long, in consequence, morality and Christian faith have been thought to be the same thing, so that 'preaching' is dismissed as telling others to be good, and 'the decent person' thought to be the real Christian. The 'establishment' of Christian faith –speaking in a general rather than a technical sense – is sometimes said to be bad for the church's integrity but good for society as a whole. This can be true only so long as what society believes Christianity to be bears some resemblance to authentic Christianity as the church understands it. That is almost certainly no longer so, at least in Britain. Perhaps it never was.

Christianity is actually no stranger to pluralism. Western Christianity, born in Judaism, grew up in the pluralist culture of the Roman Empire. We should remember that there is also an Eastern Christianity, represented by the Oriental Orthodox Christians – the Syrian, Assyrian, Armenian, Coptic and Ethiopian churches – but sadly perhaps, their historic influence on the culture of the West has been minimal. In the Roman Empire all religions had to acknowledge Roman supremacy and struggle for public acceptance in the framework of Roman law and administration. After the destruction of the empire the trustee of classical learning in the West was the church, whose monks and priests virtually moulded the medieval European mind. (In the East the trustees became the Muslims.) This grip was broken at the Reformation, and a degree of pluralism painfully re-initiated with the emergence of the Protestant churches.

The growing significance in Western life of religious traditions other than Christian marks a moment to discover again what Christianity really is. When we have got over our alarm we shall find it exhilarating, though like any worthwhile adventure, also genuinely dangerous.

But some reading this may already be impatient with the author for hanging out the Christian flag so ostentatiously. A pluralist world, some think, demands a lower confessional profile, and the history of the church's relations with those of other faiths, especially the Jewish people, suggests that Christians have little reason to desire much exposure to the gaze of the modern world. But there are two reasons for refusing this kind of obscurity. First it would be a betrayal of the world church. *Western* Christianity has indeed reflected many of the ills of Western society, and those who bore the name of Christ sometimes acted detestably in his name. But

Asian, African, and Latin-American Christians cannot be tarred with that brush. Not only Jews but black South African Christians know what it is to suffer at the hands of those who regard themselves as defending Christian civilization. Indian Christian villagers can in no sense be held responsible for the Crusades. Black American and Caribbean Christians were the victims, not the perpetrators, of the slave trade. Westerners never were the only Christians. Now they are a minority among Christians.

The second reason for setting Christianity firmly in the preface to the argument of this book is that I believe an author should make clear his presuppositions, as far as he is aware of them. Often as a reader one struggles to uncover the author's standpoint while he spends pages maintaining a facade of neutrality, pretending he presents objective facts untainted by any prior ideological commitment. In reality the facts marshalled for any argument are properly and inevitably selective, and it is always well to know on what basis the author thinks he is making his selection.

I do not imply by this any thoroughgoing relativity, that one standpoint is as good as another. I believe to be true the central assertion of Christianity, that Jesus of Nazareth died for the whole human race and now lives as its rightful sovereign. I believe this to be true, and true for everyone, not just for Christians. Naturally, therefore, I want everyone to acknowledge its truth.

Some will want to know at this point what kind of commitment this implies to a genuinely plural society. There are those who take it for granted that a whole-hearted enthusiasm for our multiracial and multifaith society will always be accompanied by a tacit agreement that we in no way seek the conversion of the other to our own point of view. 'How can you really accept Muslims or Hindus if you still want them to be different, to join your lot and be Christians? Isn't that cultural tribalism?' I could reply that many Muslims hope for the conversion of Westerners to Islam, and that some have actually taken that step, yet their commitment to a plural society goes unquestioned. The point is of course that Muslims are obviously a minority in the West, part of a whole variety of people who experience daily racial discrimination and even verbal and physical abuse. They feel isolated and vulnerable to the corrupting influences of an alien society. Christians, in contrast, are reckoned to be the vast majority, to be at home and therefore able to play the part of host. A host's task is to make his guest feel at home, not to challenge his lifestyle or religious orientation.

This sounds a persuasive line of argument until looked at in a world perspective. In the West it is true, Christians are generally numerically and institutionally more powerful than other religious groups, though the steep decline in church membership of the historic denominations has been too well documented for denial. In parts of Africa too, Christians are in a majority, as of course in Latin America and the Philippines. Elsewhere, however, especially in the Middle East, Asia and the Communist bloc, Muslims, Hindus, Buddhists or Marxists are in control. With some exceptions, notably India, the idea of a plural society has gained very little ground in these countries, and even in India growing forces for regionalism threaten it. Sikh and Hindu struggle for control of the Punjab, and Hindu and Buddhist in Sri Lanka.

The world is actually a battleground of competing ideologies and cultures and many non-Westerners see the West as bankrupt of moral and spiritual values, unable to emerge from intellectual stagnation. If Westerners simply continue to advocate peace and harmony in the plural society without offering any vision for society other than multiplicity, no one who holds more definite and coherent views is likely to be much impressed. Eventually the poverty of their vision will strike the Westerners also.

How then is it possible to affirm the value and importance for the future of a plural society, and yet to promote a Christian social and moral vision and seek to win people to it? The answer lies in the nature of the Christian message. Conversion in the Christian sense is to the living Christ, to the Scriptures which witness to him, and to the church which worships God in his name. Christian conversion is not to a particular culture or even to a set of beliefs, although it does of course take place in a particular cultural and intellectual context. Looked at in world-wide perspective there exists the most astonishing diversity of Christian life. Even in a single country like Britain there are many styles of Christian worship and different understandings of Christian belief and practice, of the correct organization of the church and its relation to the wider community.

A proper awareness of this diversity ought to reassure those who see Christian persuasiveness as a new form of imperialism. The New Testament itself records the successful struggle to prevent belief in the living Christ from being tied to the acceptance of a particular culture and an ethnic set of values. Paul fought for the freedom of non-Jewish Christians not to be compelled to observe Jewish law and customs. Tragically that freedom struggle, like others since, turned into a murderous tyranny of the victors, the non-Jewish Christians, over the people of the previously dominant culture, the Jews. But once the principle was established there was always the hope that this kind of corruption could be set aside and the proper implications of Christian freedom – for those who do not share Christian convictions as well as those who do – be put into action.

In the West that moment has finally come in the irrevocable advent of religious and cultural pluralism. For the first time in centuries Western Christians – indeed all people of whatever faith or none – are being compelled to make the difficult distinction between faith and culture. (Muslim villagers from Pakistan or Bangladesh have the same experience when they encounter Muslims from the Middle East or Europe whose understanding of Islam differs from their own in significant detail.)

Yet pluralism itself – the freedom to believe or not believe, to conform or (within proper limits) not to conform, freedom from the undue domination of one ethnic or social group – all this is continually being threatened by extremist groups of many political complexions. Western Christians exist in a precious freedom which is in part the fruit of Christian understanding. If they fail to make serious efforts to ensure that the same freedom is extended to religious minorities in the West, they need not hope that it will be long sustained for themselves. Freedom is indivisible, and belief in future will always be held in the context of a mixed society. It is important, therefore, that there should be a proper confidence in the mixed character of that society. In Jesus' parable the farmer instructed his men not to uproot the weeds which had been maliciously sown in among the wheat, lest the wheat also suffer, but to wait till they could be separated at harvest time.[1] The message stands however the wheat and the weeds are identified.

At the same time we cannot acquiesce in an understanding of pluralism which simply expects us to regard our differing theologies and ways of worship as so many private optional variations on a common theme. That common theme proves to be rather indefinite when people are asked to spell it out, but would generally be thought of as a corporate life marked by peace, prosperity, justice and compassion. Pluralism, on this reckoning, turns out to be nothing to do with final ends, on which agreement is assumed, but is a pluralism of means. In the conventional phrase, 'there are many paths to God' – 'God' standing for all that is desirable. In political vocabulary the word 'theology', used at one time by the British prime minister Harold Wilson to deride outdated socialist ideology, now often refers to any rigid political philosophy held by politicians of strong conviction and inflexible temper.

There are great difficulties in this 'non-theological' under-standing of pluralism. Religious believers of real conviction are obstinately unwilling to see their faith merely as one possible path to a secular goal. The heart of religious belief and worship is surely the giving of oneself to an ultimate being in unreserved surrender. Anything less than unconditional self-abandonment in worship implies an attempt to manipu-late divinity while the real centre of concern remains the self. This is either hypocrisy, or some attempt at magic. To the believer, then, it matters enormously what or whom he enthrones as ultimate, because that ultimate concern will be allowed and invited to shape and control his life and personal-ity, and through him that of his society. If God is God, he cannot be a means to any end, however admirable that end may seem to be in itself. This must be made clear to those who want to use religion, for example by promoting multifaith services as an exercise in community relations. The use of religion as a means to an end undermines the very character of religion itself.

In the chapters that follow I shall try to explore the question marks placed by people of other faiths over many areas of our common life in the West, and particularly in Britain. In many cases we shall want to consider their alternative patterns of thought and practice very carefully, to ask if there are not many things which we in the West, with a broadly Christian heritage, do not have to learn, unlearn and re-learn with the help of those of other faiths. I aim to be loyal to the heart of the Christian faith as I understand it while asking very seriously where we in the West may have gone wrong or need help, sometimes urgently. Others would of course make different judgements, but my own conviction is that wherever a 'better way' is found it will in fact accord with the understanding of God, life and the world revealed in Jesus Christ.

Chapter One

Education

The African or Asian student is a familiar figure in Western colleges and universities. Financed by Western scholarships, his own government or less often by his own family, he or sometimes she comes to 'take full advantage of Western education' before returning to their own country, and perhaps a distinguished career. I spent a short time as part of the very small flow in the other direction, a Western student in a Pakistani university. There I was made very conscious of the shortcomings of the Pakistani educational system, its inertia and lack of funds, and the constant disruption by political activity. There was no shortage of talent, but the problem lay elsewhere, principally in the chronic insecurity – economic and political – of the country.

With this rather jaundiced view of Pakistani education I was a bit put out to hear the views of some Pakistani parents settled in Britain about the education their children were receiving. They were not satisfied. Education was better in Pakistan. I was taken aback. Whatever the problems in the inner-city schools, I thought, they are surely better off than they would be in Pakistan. Then I listened more carefully and began to hear more clearly: the complaint was not about the *skills* their children were learning. Their point was that in Pakistan education was a matter of the whole personality, a matter of *manners* as much as skills. I thought of the traditional respect for the teacher in Eastern society and began to see the point. Their criticism was based on a completely different idea of what education should be. It was not, as they saw it, simply a matter of ensuring that children were competent in the basic skills of literacy and numeracy. They wanted children to be told how those skills should be exercised, to what use they should be put. Teaching children to think for themselves came very low on their list of priorities. What they wanted was a child learning to be familiar with all the glories of the past and its wisdom, a child who could hold his head up in the future because he knew who he was and where he belonged and to whom he owed obedience.

A Muslim educational conference held in Mecca in 1977 said the same thing:

Education should aim at the balanced growth of the total personality of Man through the training of Man's spirit, intellect, the rational self, feelings and bodily senses. Education should therefore cater for the growth of man in all its aspects: spiritual, intellectual, imaginative, physical, scientific, linguistic, both individually and collectively and motivate all these aspects towards goodness and the attainment of perfection. The ultimate aim of Muslim education lies in the realization of complete submission to Allah on the level of the individual, the community and humanity at large.[1]

Al-Attas's *Aims and Objectives of Islamic Education*[2] begins more simply: 'The aim of education in Islam is to produce a good man.' My own father, who knew nothing of Islam and had very little formal education, also believed that education and morality were intimately linked. The wide support for church schools must also owe something to the same perception that education is more than the transmission of certain mental skills. The radical philosopher Ivan Illich launched a memorable attack on the whole institution of compulsory schooling by which the pupil is

'schooled' to confuse teaching with learning, grade advancement with education, a diploma with competence, and fluency with the ability to say something new. . . most people acquire most of their knowledge outside school.[3]

Education is certainly more than what takes place in schools and colleges. Nevertheless we are stuck with schools and colleges, and the debate will continue about just what should go on in them. People of minority faiths and ethnic groups will have sharp perceptions about what is happening and in their opinion ought to happen, precisely because they are minorities and see things from a different angle to the majority – a point of view less blurred by familiarity. They should be heard, for all our sakes.

One way of describing this debate in education is in terms of 'transmission' and 'transformation'. Is the task of education

the transmission to the next generation of the skills and
knowledge which have been acquired and valued in previous
generations? Or is it rather to begin a radical change in society
itself through a new approach with those who will eventually
lead it? Are the children to be prepared for the world as it has
been or as it might become? Some thinkers put the same basic
question by asking whether education is essentially about
'banking' the skills and knowledge a child will need to draw
on for the rest of his life; or whether it is about learning to
think independently, to pose and solve problems so that he
can be confident of dealing with anything that turns up.

If they were asked to take part in such an argument, our
Pakistani parents mentioned above would almost certainly
come down on the 'transmission'/'banking' side, although
they would want to put more than merely skills and knowledge into the bank. They would want to add what the
Muslim educational conference called 'man becoming aware
of his destiny as the vice-regent of God on earth'. They would
not be afraid to speak of 'moulding' and 'shaping' a child, or
directing him in the way that he should go. Others would call
that 'indoctrination', and regard it as an infringement of the
proper freedom of the child to develop in his own way, free
from such 'ideological' influences.

It is an open question whether the 'transmissionist' or the
'transformationist' school of thought is more likely to indoctrinate children. Critics of the transmissionist school have
maintained that 'too often this heritage has merely represented the fossilized formulations of the values and interests
of the middle class'.[4] If education is 'initiation into worthwhile
areas of knowledge', who decides what is worthwhile? 'Trans-
formationists' themselves sometimes see the classroom as a
'vital powerhouse for the teacher committed to the socialist
transformation of society and the fight against racism'.[5] If
indoctrination is wrong, then it is wrong to indoctrinate
children even against racism. Is the child merely to be an
object to be shaped in accordance with certain ends, however
admirable those ends may be? Can he not become the subject
of his own development? Or is that hopelessly naive?

Beyond this basic question of what *kind* of education is
being given, is the question of what *content* should be dealt

with. It is obvious that no country can any longer afford to educate its children as though, for example, British literature was the only literature of real quality, British (or more likely English) history was the only history that mattered, and the Western way of life the only desirable one. Yet there is plenty of evidence to show that in many of the textbooks used in schools in Britain, Australia and the United States today is embedded a subtle, and sometimes blatant devaluation of non-Western cultures. Among many examples from books used in British schools today we can take two from history texts:

> . . . the people of Britain were great merchants and explorers. As a result, British colonies were set up all over the world. In some colonies, like Canada, Australia and New Zealand there were only white people and a few coloured people. In India and Africa, there were coloured people who had always lived there and only a few British people. This difference was important. It meant that lands like Canada obtained the right to govern itself quite soon, and became the equal of Britain, the Motherland.

Clearly this passage can be read in two ways, either as a neutral statement of fact, or as conveying the clear message of African and Asian inferiority, but the idea of Britain as the motherland suggests, at least, a mother who has favourite children. The child image recurs in another book about India:

> With British rule came British law, British education and British customs, and most important of all the British language. This more than anything else helped to unite the divided races of India. . . As the peoples of India became more united they became conscious of themselves as a nation. . . They became proud of their past, their customs and their religions. . . Soon they wanted to rule themselves. This was very natural. Just as children grow up and in the end want to rule their own lives, so with people.[6]

This patronizing account of the Indian struggle for independence turns men of the stature of Gandhi and Nehru into rebellious adolescents.

In 1758 the Swedish natural scientist Carl von Linné defined four races in humanity:

–American Indian: reddish, tall, choleric and stubborn
–European: white, muscular, agile and inventive
–Asian: yellow, melancholy, unyielding and stingy
–African: black, phlegmatic, easy-going, indolent and drowsy[7]

Ridiculous as such ideas appear today, they still recur in some books used in schools. African people live in 'huts' rather than 'homes', their racial groupings are called 'tribes', and their languages 'dialects'. Natives are 'killed', while settlers are 'massacred'; Third World countries are 'uncivilized', 'backward' or 'heathen'. History and geography are the main subjects to come under fire here, but issues of development and economics, languages, literature and religious education are all involved.

People often express the feeling that while such language is understandably offensive to those who live in the Third World, it does not need to be taken with too much seriousness elsewhere. Multiracial and multicultural concerns, they imply, are only the business of those who live in that kind of society. 'We don't have that problem here.' Such attitudes are often fuelled by a concern that children could lose all understanding of their own culture. A history professor from St Andrew's University, Scotland, has written, uncompromisingly, that

There is no point in giving children potted histories of Africa or America on the plea that it broadens the mind or fosters international understanding if it leaves them in ignorance of how our own complex and delicately balanced society came into being. *As for those of different cultural backgrounds, the sooner they are assimilated the better.* (my italics)[8]

But surely, in the last quarter of the twentieth century it is absurd and dangerous to allow education to be preoccupied with one particular set of national values and the history of one particular nation. There must be a proper recognition of the interdependence of every national community, and access given to accurate information about the cultures of other societies. Like other Western nations, Britain now contains a large variety of social and ethnic groups. This variety should be evident in the visual material, the stories and information offered to children, and people from minority groups should not be insulted by their portrayal in some stereotyped form instead of as the individuals they are.

It must be recognized, however, that this is a highly complex and contentious issue to which the whole of this book could easily be given over. Parents naturally feel very strongly about the shaping of their children's minds which takes place in school, and in many cases already feel the gulf between their children's education and their own. The 'addition', as they see it, of a lot more 'irrelevant' information geared to the needs of specific minorities is very threatening. In 1977 a British government Green Paper entitled *Education in Schools: A Consultative Document* argued that

> Our society is a multi-cultural, multi-racial one and the curriculum should reflect a sympathetic understanding of the different cultures and races that now make up our society. . . the curriculum of schools must reflect the needs of this new Britain.[9]

But it seems that this recommendation is only very slowly being recognized and implemented, for once the prejudicial attitudes referred to above have been eliminated, it is still not easy to determine the appropriate balance of different cultural elements in a multicultural education. The cultures of the newly immigrant communities are changing as well as that of the 'host' culture, and it does no child a service to be educated into the culture of its parents' generation if that culture is disappearing. It is also likely, unless the multicultural concept is introduced into schools with particular thoroughness and care that its effect could be the opposite of that intended. Parents and children from the majority community, resentful at the imposition of a new educational philosophy clumsily introduced, could react by refusing any new knowledge or perspective, and take out their anger on the ethnic minority people they know. Some racist groups would like nothing better.

Similar problems arise with the teaching of the languages of ethnic minority groups. Some British examples would be Urdu, Punjabi and Bengali, languages with long histories, large populations and extensive literatures. In some parts of Wales education has been carried on for many years wholly or partly in Welsh, and yet there is considerable resistance to acknowledging the languages of South Asia as a personal and national asset. A House of Commons Affairs Committee reported in 1981 on teaching in Urdu or Punjabi or other languages that

> We are not convinced either that a local education authority is under any obligation to provide mother-tongue teaching or that it is necessarily in the general interest that they should do so.[10]

The principal stimulus to mother tongue teaching in Britain has undoubtedly been the European Economic Community's Directive on the Education of Migrant Workers' Children, 1977, which envisaged a somewhat different situation from the British one.[11]

But the most obvious changes in school syllabus connected with the growth of a multiracial and multifaith society in Britain have been those in religious education. Religious education was beginning to change already under the stimulus of Harold Loukes and Ronald Goldman, who pointed out that much of what was taught in religious education was way beyond the experience of children, and far more suited to an adult understanding. Teaching too much too soon could, and they reckoned did, make children unwilling to re-examine at a later age material which bored them when young. But it was the growing presence of young Muslims, Hindus and Sikhs in British schools which created an apparently unanswerable argument for the radical move away from a syllabus centred on the Bible to what might be called Religious Studies. The present situation is extremely varied. According to Owen Cole, one of the most distinguished pioneers in religious education:

> Religion in school might be described as an appendix without a body. Once the body was definite, it was the Bible, but in many schools today the Judaeo-Christian scriptures have themselves become an appendix at the end of a life-theme, or an afterthought to Hinduism or one of the other Eastern faiths.[12]

One common characteristic, however, is the attempt to include the study of at least one world religion in addition to Christianity, and it is important to notice that this attempt has been made in rural areas almost as much as in the big cities where there are concentrations of ethnic minorities.

It is worth noticing at this point that the earlier concentration on the Bible was itself the outcome of much controversy about denominational Christian teaching. It was felt in 1944 that rather than risk endless arguments about particular interpretations of the Christian faith it would be better to focus on the scriptures which all Christians agreed to be central to their faith. Denominational schools (Voluntary Aided schools) were free to teach according to their own particular emphasis. But the institutional decline of the churches in the fifties and sixties and early seventies meant that increasing numbers of children had no experience of a living Christian community for whom the Bible was a living text. Religious education classes based on it became more and more unreal, since it related to nothing else in their daily lives. At the same time the attempt to continue worship in school assembly met the problem that most had no experience of worship at all, and could not be expected to learn at school what elsewhere in the world is almost universally taught at home, at the mother's knee.

In this situation some have clutched at world faiths as at a straw in answer to the criticisms of pupils, parents and teachers alike. Yet the situation is not necessarily altered by teaching world faiths. Edward Hulmes writes:

New syllabuses, however imaginative their construction, will not, of themselves, change the situation. As one teacher put it to me recently with devastating simplicity, 'After three years of world religions the children are just as bored as they were with Christianity. What are we going to do about *that*?'[13]

Others see the situation much more positively. Owen Cole has written recently that 'my conviction that Religious Education has perhaps the greatest contribution to make in educating everyone for the multi-cultural reality has increased, not diminished.'[14]

Obviously everything depends on the enthusiasm and skill of the teacher, and his or her ability to relate religious education to the world both teacher and pupils are living in. As some have pointed out, religious education may be regarded as a 'Cinderella' subject but it was Cinderella who eventually married the prince, and not her ugly sisters. What better education could there be than the careful, sympathetic study of the great convictions at the heart of the world's different cultures? Nevertheless at this point we encounter considerable problems. In what spirit, and with what presuppositions is this study to be conducted? Can one agree merely to 'study' God? If genuinely ultimate questions are being handled can any teacher pretend to be neutral or objective about them? Against this it has been urged that teachers are not there to indoctrinate children or 'nurture' them in any one religious or secular philosophy, but to provide them with the intellectual equipment and basic information they need to make up their own minds. The question is whether this attitude, itself part of a certain philosophical outlook, is appropriate to the teaching of religious studies.

It is not only people of committed Christian faith who have complained that current religious education is inadequate for a proper understanding of religious faith. Even more vigorous complaints have come from Muslims, Sikhs and Hindus about the way their faiths are taught in the British classroom. The best and sincerest efforts of teachers to teach world faiths are often regarded by such parents as misrepresenting their faith. Muslims in particular frequently complain that what is taught in schools as Islam is not recognizable as such by the Muslim community. The tradition of historical and critical inquiry, to which the Bible has been subjected for over 100 years, is felt to be quite foreign to the spirit of Islam, and Muslims generally distrust the academic studies of Western 'orientalists' who advise teachers on Islam.

Islam poses a particular problem here since Muslims usually refuse to divide life into 'sacred' and 'secular' departments, and insist that all life must be given in *islam* (surrender) to God. In other words all education should be religious in spirit, because religion cannot be confined to a slot called 'religious education'. In a Muslim/Christian educational conference in 1981 it was suggested that in the situation of the 1980s Islam would have to be taught to non-Muslim children by non-Muslim teachers (as part of their general education if nothing else), but that such a presentation would be unlikely to satisfy Muslims themselves. A different kind of material on Islam was needed for Muslim children.

This brings us back to the complaints of Pakistani parents in Britain about the educational system as a whole. They dislike its secular spirit and the absence of any overarching religious principle. They particularly dislike the separation which tends to be made between religious studies and morality – a favourite theme of humanists. Muslims, Hindus, Sikhs and Jews are at one in rejecting a secular base for ethics. One effect of this is a distaste for sex education as practised in the West. *The Muslim Guide* says:

> Islam of course does not stand for ignorance and has its own method of sex education. But this is entirely different from what is practised as sex education in schools today. . . Muslim parents argue that the sex education as taught in the West will lead to moral degradation of their children. . . Muslim students should not be given any sex education as Islam does not approve of any practical demonstration of sex organs or sex play.[15]

Most people of other faiths would agree that sex education cannot be separated from religion.

Again and again in the subjects dealt with in this book we shall come across the conviction that the West has divided life up into separate bits, so that the body and its needs have been reduced to a series of mechanisms, and the wholeness of life is lost. Some would relate this to a dualism of mind and body, spirit and matter, which has been characteristic (it is claimed) of the Western world since Descartes. This division has been enormously successful in developing technology and scientific discovery, but has failed to enable the development of the human spirit in anything like the same degree. The result has been a soulless, exploitative capitalism or Marxism, and scientists who take no responsibility for the subsequent use of their work – whether it is in nuclear physics or genetic engineering. Now even in pure science, in subatomic physics for example, the Cartesian idea that the observer is totally separate from the object he studies was discredited by the work of Einstein and subsequent physicists. Parents from rural Pakistan will know nothing of this, or the complaint that the *uni*versity of today has lost any sense of the unity of knowledge and become a *multi*versity, but they have an instinctive feeling that they have lost something very precious, that life has become atomized. In the words so often quoted from Yeats:

Things fall apart; the centre cannot hold;
Mere anarchy is loosed upon the world.

It is in this context that we need to understand the desire of many Muslim and Sikh parents in Britain for voluntary aided Muslim or Sikh schools within the state-maintained sector, on the model of the Church of England, Roman Catholic and Jewish schools already established. Church involvement in British education goes back to the days when the only schools were either provided by the church or by pious Christian benefactors on an explicitly religious foundation. The oldest British universities have similar origins. Consequently the church's concern for education has from the beginning been for the nation as a whole, and not merely the nurture of a particular group within it. But can any 'confessional' school realistically prepare children for a multicultural society? Is not the very concept an anachronism? Yet the fact is that, particularly at secondary level, Church of England schools at least are very popular, often encountering great problems over admissions procedure because they are over-subscribed. What is more, many Muslim, Sikh and Hindu parents send their children to these schools, sometimes because they are the only single-sex schools available, but also because they offer a religious framework for all their teaching. It is clear that confessional schools can be justified on the grounds of diversity in education, provided they also avoid the creation of a ghetto mentality. Some parents, however, clearly desire to send their children to a church school because it is perceived as a 'white' school, where contact with ethnic minority children and affairs can be avoided.

On the grounds of educational diversity and common justice it is difficult to deny to religious minorities the same facility that is enjoyed by the churches and the Jewish community. In fact there appears to be no legal obstacle to doing so provided it can be shown that there are sufficient parents ready to support such schools, and that appropriate staff and facilities can be found. The Mecca Conference of 1977, already referred to, made clear the Muslim desire that 'the Divine revelation presented in the Qur'an and Sunnah' together with 'acquired' (what we might call 'secular') knowledge

> must be made obligatory to all Muslims at all levels of the educational system from the highest to the lowest. . . This, along with the compulsory teaching of Arabic, should form the major section of the core curriculum. These two alone can sustain Islamic civilization and preserve the identity of the Muslims.[16]

Such a programme can obviously be made available only in a school run by Muslims. Yet even Muslim control will not ensure it. Some Muslims have distinguished between 'Muslim schools' which are merely run and staffed by Muslims and have Muslim pupils, and 'Islamic schools' where the whole character of the teaching is moulded by Islamic precept. They would go on to question whether many 'Islamic schools' exist even in the Muslim world, so powerful has been the influence of Western educational models.

Others, Muslim and non-Muslim, ask how wise it is to create ghetto schools where children from one religious community never have the opportunity to mix with those from others. The young Muslims of Bradford have shown themselves well aware of this danger in opposing the demand of some of their elders for Muslim schools in the city. Occasionally the results of the segregated education of Northern Ireland are held up as a warning.[17] It is often pointed out that the creation of Muslim or Sikh schools will separate children on the basis of religion, but also effectively on the basis of skin-colour. Some young Muslims have expressed the fear that such schools would become known as 'immigrant schools' or even 'wog schools'.[18] A Church of England discussion paper on the subject asks 'Should the price paid for a sustaining of cultural identity and personal dignity be *isolation*?'[19]

A particular issue here is the education of secondary-age Muslim girls, some of whom are at present illegally withheld from schools by their parents, because there is no local single-sex school for them, or because their parents wish to avoid any possibility of contact with the opposite sex outside the family. Would it be right to allow the creation of Muslim girls' secondary schools where Muslim girls would be effectively segregated on the basis of religion, colour and sex? Such schools might well be difficult to staff also.

But not all Muslims, as we have seen, demand Muslim schools. *The Muslim Guide*, prepared by a group of Muslim scholars for 'teachers, employers, community workers and social administrators in Britain' does not refer to the issue at all in its section on the Muslim child at school. But it does list fourteen recommendations which it believes may 'occasion some initial inconvenience and slight reorganization', but which will pay dividends in the removal of conflict and tension caused at present by the obstacles in the way of Muslim children observing their religion. It is worth quoting them in full:

1. Muslim teachers in schools with a high percentage of Muslim pupils could be asked to volunteer to act as religious instruction co-ordinators and welfare officers/consultants on problems which appear to be aided by an empirical knowledge of Islam.

2. Time and classrooms allocated for religious instruction of Muslim pupils by Muslim teachers in schools.

3. Provision of a prayer room, adjacent to washing facilities for congregational worship.

4. Invitations to *imams* and Islamic scholars to visit and give talks in school.

5. In social studies and in general religious studies, allowing Muslims, rather than non-Muslims, to present Islam to the school generally, with the promotion of religious tolerance and understanding in view.

6. Arrangements for non-Muslim pupils to visit the Mosques.

7. Enlisting the support of a Muslim teacher to be responsible for encouraging Muslim parents to attend parent–teacher meetings, and having interpreters in Asian languages available to assist parents in discussing the educational programme and problems of their pupils.

8. Inviting *imams* and Muslim scholars to accept positions on school, college and youth centre management committees.

9. Allow Muslim children to withdraw from collective worship and morning assemblies, where they are Christian-orientated.

10. Allowing Muslim boys and girls to be absent from sex education classes.

11. In institutions and organizations with a high percentage of Muslims, it may not be economically unfeasible to employ a full or part-time cook and have a separate cooking unit.

12. The preparation of a wide range of vegetarian dishes – salads, cheese and mushroom omelettes, fish, rice, macaroni, spaghetti and boiled eggs etc.

13. In schools, it is particularly important that the children are not placed in circumstances in which they are forced either to eat unlawful food or go hungry.

14. In cookery classes, Muslim pupils must not be allowed to prepare meals from pork or other unlawful ingredients.[20]

The Muslim Guide says that some of these recommendations are already being followed and obviously some of them would suggest themselves to sensitive head teachers whose schools contained large numbers of Muslim children. Others, no. 10 perhaps, would create real difficulties.

Some of the schools which already contain, or in future might contain, large numbers of Muslim children and children of Hindu and Sikh faith, are voluntary aided church schools. The situation has arisen because the original area served by the school now has a high proportion of children of Asian origin. If the school insists on taking only Christian children it is in danger of becoming a white school, open to the charge of racism. It would also fail to serve the neighbourhood in which it is set. In addition, Asian parents of all faiths often desire the religious outlook and philosophy of such schools for their own children, though they do not want any change in the religious identity of their children. Where such schools are single-sex and have a reputation for firm discipline there are additional reasons for Asian approval. The church school is then faced with the task of adjusting to the presence of children whose parents approve the religious basis of the school, but not the involvement of their children in explicitly Christian activities.

How many of The Muslim Guide's recommendations will a church school feel able to follow? If no. 9 were observed it might in some cases have the effect of totally altering the

whole character of the school. On the other hand the adjustment of school assembly worship in order to make Muslims
feel at home in it might lead either to mere moral exhortation
which is not worship at all, or else a watering down of
Christian faith to a theistic worship which makes Christians
feel they have betrayed their Lord. Much more thought needs
to be given to what worship really is in the understanding of
Christians and those of other faiths, and whether the captive
audience of a school can ever be said to be truly worshipping.
Since all formal Muslim worship is carried out in Arabic, Sikh
worship in Punjabi, and much Hindu worship in Sanskrit,
worship in English is often identified as Christian, and
however 'adjusted' will be regarded by some as improper for
their children.

Christians too respond in different ways to the situation.
Some feel that the Christian basis of a church school should be
explicit, carefully explained to parents and accepted by them
as the ethos of the school before their children are admitted. If
insufficient parents are prepared to accept it then the school
should be handed over completely to the local education
authority. Others sympathize with the sincere concern of the
Muslim, Sikh or Hindu parents for the religious education of
their children and are prepared to allow, and even organize
the separate instruction of such children by teachers recognized by the different faith communities. Still others hope to
provide a religious and general education in which it is
possible for people of all faiths and cultures to share and be
mutually enriched, without pretending that there is some easy
and painless way of reconciling the different (many would say
'incompatible') religious claims to truth.

Recently it has been suggested that in some of those Church
of England voluntary aided schools where there is at present
actually a majority of children of other faiths (in some cases as
high as 80 per cent or 90 per cent of the total), control over the
school might be offered to representatives of other faiths for an
agreed period. If it be objected that this would be a denial of
Trust deeds, 'let it be said that if reconciliation of man with
man (as well as man with God) is truly part of the redemptive
process and is a worthy doctrine, then to exemplify that
doctrine in the life of the school can hardly be a denial of

trust.'[21]

Some reading these pages may have become impatient with the discussion of problems and situations peculiar to Britain. It is, however, the depth of the historic involvement of the church in British life that creates such problems in a pluralist society. Little, it seems to me, is to be gained by a withdrawal from them, by a policy of maintaining the purity of the faith by exclusiveness. 'Those who claim that through the costly act of self-giving by Christ a process of reconciliation has begun in which Christians strive to break barriers, should shun exclusiveness.'[22] At the same time engagement with such issues drives us back into our basic theological understanding of what Christian faith is all about. Surely none of us can object to that.

Chapter Two

Blessing and Refuge

When I try to explain my job to people with no close connection to the churches, and talk about motivating Christians to meet people of other faiths, and learn more about those faiths, the response is often on the lines of 'Oh, you're trying to bring all the religions together – what a good idea.' And then, of course, I have to start all over again. For in our pluralist society people might be divided almost equally between those who think that one day – perhaps sooner than we think – we shall end up with one religion, and those that take the real differences between faiths much more seriously.

Both groups are faced with the prospect of people of different faiths worshipping together. The first group is enthusiastic about it, the second is in varying degrees hesitant or opposed. Nevertheless the pressure is on in some schools and colleges to bring people together in joint acts of worship, and many would ask 'Can we not express our basic religious hope and belief in common? Is there no possibility of finding together some expression of our common belief in a spiritual dimension to life – in the Transcendent?' Such a question becomes particularly acute when it is asked by the representatives of the whole local or national community, as in the various attempts to construct a civic service with a feel for other faiths than the traditional Christian one, or in the annual Commonwealth Day service in Westminister Abbey.

Christians themselves differ sharply about the propriety of such occasions, some feeling that profound convictions are in danger of being sacrificed to a superficial and unreal unity. Others feel that there are no adequate grounds for excluding the valid expressions of another culture, based on religion like all culture, at an occasion which is designed to express the unity of all citizens. One group feels that faith is being sacrificed to political expediency (and not only Christians would look at it this way), the other that religion is once again being allowed to divide people, and even used as a means of perpetuating the superiority of a particular culture. There is no simple answer to such religio-political questions. If there is to be a chaplain to the House of Commons, who begins each day's proceedings with prayer, is there any reason why it should not on occasion be a Jewish rabbi? There are many Jews in the House of Commons. There are not yet Muslim, Sikh or Hindu members, yet considering the presence in the general population of large minorities of such people, is it not a form of discrimination to exclude their representative religious leaders from occasional opportunities of serving in a similar way?

Some of the political questions of Christian 'establishment' must be taken up later, but here it may be of value to examine more closely what we mean by the whole concept of 'worship'. The English word has no exact equivalent in a number of other languages, and like all words is gradually changing its meaning. Older usage is still reflected in the archaic title 'Your Worship', and in the promise of the older form of the marriage service: 'With my body I thee worship.' Here the dominant notion is of respect in a very high degree, the giving of 'worth'. But particularly in the marriage vow, more is implied – the giving of oneself in unconditional love or surrender. So the Authorized King James Version of the Bible consistently translates the Greek word *proskuneo* – literally, to kiss the hand towards, or to fall down before (kissing the earth or the feet) – but always before God, or God's instrument, for example angels, Moses, the prophets, Jesus. The New Testament, with a single exception,[1] restricts the use of the word to God, Jesus and (in temptation) the devil. When John the Seer is moved to prostrate himself before the angel he is told not to, since the angel is simply a fellow servant.[2]

Both the New Testament (compared to the Old) and modern English usage have tended to confine the use of the word to God alone, or God-as-known-in-Jesus. But with the growth in Western secularity, the idea and experience of worship have become more and more remote to many people. Only a minority in Britain worship at all – in the modern sense of the word – with any regularity, and for the majority the only experience of worship is some long-forgotten series of school assemblies. Yet it seems unlikely that so deep an instinct can be lost altogether. If people no longer – in any literal sense – bow down before images or symbols of divinity, should we still assume that they do not wholeheartedly give themselves to anything? That not only has God disappeared from their lives without trace, but also that nothing has taken his place? Some indeed have a real sense that God has gone into hiding:

It is this great absence
that is like a presence, that compels
me to address it without hope
of a reply. It is a room I enter
from which someone has just
gone.[3]

R.S. Thomas is wrestling here, as so often, with the problems of prayer. The fact is, though few would admit to taking part in any kind of regular worship, a great many people do pray in times of crisis, or just when they want something very badly. But prayer, though it may be the heart of worship, is not the whole of it. I want to suggest three elements to worship, three instincts in human nature which are very deep and must be satisfied. They are the need for approval, for encouragement, for blessing, for good luck, success – however it is expressed: the need for protection, for refuge, for security, for a defence of some sort against all the ills that life can throw at us: and the need for a cause, a love, a person or an ideal big enough to demand all we have and all we are, something or someone which will not let us down by ever being less than everything to us. It is perhaps the absence of any true satisfaction for that third need which brings about the sense of flatness, of desertion, of somehow having been cheated, which is so characteristic of the late twentieth century in the West.

He is a religious man.
How often I have heard him say,
looking around him with his worried eyes
at the emptiness: There must be something.[4]

If, however, the need for a cause or a god is not satisfied, the searchers have still to find some answer to the needs which I have called the need for blessing and the need for refuge. The need for refuge or protection is perhaps the more obvious one in the life of the individual. Even modern Western man in his comparative freedom from poverty, sickness and the violent attack of enemies, still needs protection from a sense of failure and worthlessness or shame, from a purposeless existence and even from nameless evil. Some find their fears summed up in the haunting reality of death. Others fling themselves into pleasures or activities so as not to identify their fears.

As we think of today's plural societies, one of the most poignant fears to come to mind is that of people at sea in a strange environment. A recent publication describes the acute anxiety of Turkish mothers newly resident in Sweden when blue-eyed, fair-haired Swedish nurses openly admire and praise their new-born babies and young children. In central Anatolia the unusual person who has blue eyes and fair hair is believed to be able to transmit *nazar*, or the evil eye of envy. A jealous glance is sufficient to activate this potent source of ill, and expressions of praise and admiration are generally received by parents with the neutralizing expression 'mash Allah' ('It's as God wills').

> (Turkish women from Kulu) often display a negative attitude to their children. They will say that a child is ugly or has some other fault and handle it roughly rather than voicing any praise and being gentle. By taking every conceivable precaution, they can also avoid any blame should something happen to the child – they know they have done everything to protect it.[5]

In contrast, the Swedish medical staff appear to these women to understand nothing. The Turkish women complain:

> At the hospital they harm the children with their admiring looks and words. They are forever saying out loud that the children are so splendid and grand without knowing how to protect them from *nazar*.[6]

The Turkish women themselves go to great lengths to obtain amulets, or take ritual baths or dress the child unattractively in order to divert the attention of the evil eye.

In Western minds this is the wildest superstition, but it is important to recognize that a belief in the evil eye is very widespread in the developing world, and has its origins long before Christianity or Islam. The Qur'an, moreover, appears to confirm its reality in the penultimate sura:

> Say: I seek refuge in the Lord of Daybreak
> From the evil of that which He created;
> From the evil of the darkness when it is intense,

And from the evil of malignant witchcraft,
And from the evil of the envier when he envieth.[7]
For these Turkish women, and the millions of men and
women all over the Islamic world, the assurance of protection
afforded by the Qur'an is enough to justify the writing of
verses from it (such as this one) on amulets worn round the
neck, the drinking of water in which the ink of such verses has
been washed off, and the inhaling of smoke from the burning
of paper on which they have been written.

Islamic orthodoxy has always condemned such practices,
but this has not been enough to prevent them. It may be
sufficient for the learned commentators like Baidawi to write
of this Qur'anic passage that 'He who is competent to dispel
the darkness of night from this world is competent also to
dispel the fears of the one who seeks refuge with Him.'[8] But
the illiterate peasant seeks more concrete reassurance. Living
less in his head, less skilled at handling the currency of
concepts and ideas, he looks for a word from God which he
can touch and even take into his own body. Especially if the
sacred language is not his mother tongue, it is not enough for
him to memorize the verses, to combat the *idea* of evil. He
wants to make them part of himself, taking refuge in God from
its reality. Christians may be reminded of the instruction to
eat the scroll containing the words of God given to Ezekiel[9]
and to John the Seer.[10] Of course this may be a mere attempt
at magic among many Muslims, or a simple-minded supposition that the wonder (to the illiterate) of meaning conveyed by
pen and ink on paper can protect against accident, ill-will and
disease. But at its best it is a deliberate taking refuge with
God, as a common name for the amulet (*ta'widh* or *taveez*
meaning 'refuge') shows. At all times it is a more serious affair
than the lucky charms and pendant crosses worn by many
Western girls, or the talismans carried by many of our top
sportsmen into their competitions.

Of course the religious symbol, from every tradition, may
come to be thought of as significant in itself, no longer the
vehicle for the divine power, but having some kind of life of its
own. It is important for Christians to recall that this can
happen to symbols precious to themselves, even the symbol of
the cross. In the museum in Lahore, made famous as the

'wonder-house' of Rudyard Kipling's *Kim*, there is today the old bronze statue of Queen Victoria, which used to stand at a prominent site in the city. At the time of Pakistan's independence it was carefully removed to the museum, no doubt as a way of saying that the old imperial rule was now part of history. That must have been an emotional moment, yet the statue is undamaged, except for one thing. Victoria is seated, holding the orb, and the cross on top of the orb has been broken off. This could be understood as Muslim objection to the whole teaching of the cross of Christ, but it could equally well be a protest against the use of the sign of the cross to express political domination. The British Raj was not a particularly religious affair, but the memory of Crusades and imposing ecclesiastical buildings and army chaplains had associated the cross with a whole string of deeply-felt grievances, as well of course as some benefits and virtues. We cannot suppose that while the religious symbols of other traditions are open to abuse our own somehow remain inviolate. The Protestant Reformation itself had much to say about the use and abuse of religious symbols.

But what of the evil eye itself, or the host of evil spirits that swarm in some imaginations? Anthropologists have been at pains in recent years to make us realize that the supposition of evil spirit activity is rarely or never understood as a complete explanation for some misfortune. It takes its place alongside Western scientific explanations for disease and accident as an interpretation of the event at a deeper level. Technical information, in terms of bacteria and other micro-organisms, is acknowledged, but deeper questions remain. As Mary Douglas writes of the Azande people of the Sudan:

> When technical information has been exhausted, curiosity turns instead to focus on the involvement of a particular person with the universe. Why did it have to happen to him? What can he do to prevent misfortune? Is it anyone's fault?. . . Why did this farmer's crops fail and not his neighbour's? Why did this man get gored by a wild buffalo and not another of his hunting party?[11]

In face of such questions the Western instinct is to press for further information of a technical sort. Is this farmer's land more fertile than his neighbour's? Does he have easier access

to water? Is he more assiduous in cultivating it than his
neighbour? Was the man who was gored careless or unskilled
in hunting? When the answers fail we are likely to say 'Well,
he was simply unlucky', which is really no explanation at all.
If anything the answer 'luck' says much less and is much less
satisfying than the answer 'evil eye'. Bishop Lesslie Newbigin,
calling for a revision of many Western assumptions about our
'enlightenment' recounts his injury in a bus accident in India,
an injury that happened soon after his arrival as a missionary
and which incapacitated him for two years.

How to 'explain' it? The Indian pastor said: 'It is the will of
God.' A Hindu would have said: 'The karma of your former
lives has caught up with you.' In some cultures the explanation would be that an enemy had put a curse on me. If I,
as an 'enlightened' European, had said that it was because
the brakes were not working properly, that would have been
–for the others – no explanation at all. It would have been
simply a re-statement of what had to be explained.[12]

Every culture has its own framework of explanation to enable
people to make sense of what happens to them. As we look
closely at the more 'religious' or 'superstitious' frameworks
used by other people, we begin to see our own in a new light.
It may appear mechanistic, atomized, impersonal, refusing to
see deeper questions in daily events or to recognize a personal
will behind the things that happen. The way in which the
Turkish women in Sweden explained accidents reminded
their sociologist of Evans-Pritchard's accounts of the Azande,
a 'primitive' people. A boy has fallen as he ran down a
staircase that has a faulty step. Why?

The boy has run up and down the stairs many times before
now, suddenly, he falls. Why? Because he ran too fast? No,
he ran no faster than usual. Because the step is faulty? It's
been that way a long time and he has not tripped before. It
must have been some evil force that caused the boy to trip
and hurt himself on this particular occasion.[13]

It seems to me particularly significant that the evil eye is
associated most closely with jealousy, with 'the envier when
he envieth', with the outward pretence of approval and
admiration contrasting with inward hatred and the desire to
destroy, or seize for oneself. Nothing of course is more

damaging to personal relations than envy and the suspicion of it. Mary Douglas notes that ever since Levy-Bruhl's *Primitives and the Supernatural* (1936) anthropologists have studied 'the strenuous efforts that are made to bring the inward heart and mind into line with the public act' in so-called 'primitive' societies.[14] External behaviour should match the secret emotions, or the world is out of joint and trouble will occur. In the primal crime the death of Abel comes about through Cain's jealousy.

> The Lord said to Cain, 'Why are you so angry and cast down? If you do well you are accepted; if not, sin is a demon crouching at the door. It shall be eager for you but you must master it.[15]

Jealousy is evidence of a deep disorder in the world, before which human beings can only run for refuge to the strongest power they know, which may be the Qur'an, or the power brought about through sacrifice, or the power of a holy person (usually, but not always, male). In each case it is a divine power which they seek through the agency of some assured, approved text or rite or man.

The text or the rite have the sanction of tradition, maybe of centuries. But how does the holy man arise? As anthropologists see it, the witch or sorcerer becomes known when someone against whom he or she has an evident grudge falls prey to some misfortune. Similarly, a person with a reputation for learning and piety is suddenly associated with a piece of unusual good fortune. Note how these events become 'personalized' in the minds of observers. Once suggested, the saint's reputation is self-validating, just as the 'witches' of sixteenth and seventeenth-century Europe were confirmed in their reputation with every disaster that befell their neighbours.[16]

In Muslim tradition the saint is thought to possess *baraka* (literally 'blessing'), a superabundance of divine power which is available through physical contact with him as though he were electrically charged. His glance, his touch, even his clothes, hair clippings or nail parings have the power to bless, produce healing and work miracles. Even after his death, those who come to pray at his grave are sure of an answer, for spiritual power inheres the place where his body rests. Lest we think this peculiar to Islam, let me quote a typical passage from Bede's great *History of the English Church and People*, which abounds in the miracles wrought at the tombs of saints, and by their bodily touch, whether alive or dead:

> Oswald's great devotion and faith in God was made evident by the miracles that took place after his death. For at the place where he was killed fighting for his country against the heathen, sick men and beasts are healed to this day. Many people took earth from the place where his body fell, and put it in water, from which sick folk who drank it received great benefit.[17]

It is doubtful whether Muslim saints dying in England today would bring about the same devotion and apparent effect seen today in Muslim countries or in the time of Bede in England itself. Even the shrine of the Virgin at Walsingham cannot begin to match the attraction exercised by, for example the shrine of Data Ganj Bakhsh in Lahore, though perhaps Lourdes may.

Here, however, an issue arises which cannot be side-stepped. If the spiritual power exercised by some living people or at some places is real, and not just an illusion, how do we regard it? For the sceptic, of course, the question does not arise, for he classes such 'events' as illusory, to be explained by some natural, if unknown, occurrence, or by 'sheer coincidence'. 'Coincidence' is actually no more of an explanation than 'luck' to those who cannot accept a fortuitous world of random happenings. But to the religious believer who does see the world and human history as essentially a unity, for whom there is a sense of purpose in the universe, the question becomes acute: is this display of spiritual power benign or does it come from some evil source? Here I believe it is worth bearing in mind the words of Jesus when he was accused of healing people by means of evil powers. He reasons with his opponents that Satan, being evil, can have no interest in healing, since he is himself the cause of sickness and psychological bondage.

> If it is Satan who casts out Satan, Satan is divided against himself; how then can his kingdom stand? And if it is by Beelzebub that I cast out devils, *by whom do your own people drive them out?* If this is your argument, they themselves will refute you.[18] (my italics)

Attention is usually focussed by New Testament commentators on the logic of Jesus' reply where his own activities are concerned. But I am interested in the supplementary application of the same basic argument to those exorcists and healers recognized as genuinely effective by his opponents. If healing is genuinely effective, can it ever be brought about by evil means? This seems to be the major question that Jesus is asking. 'You can tell a tree by its fruit' he goes on to argue.[19] The power and the effectiveness of Jesus' miracles alarmed his critics, who felt driven to deny the evidence of their own senses. Jesus warns them that there is no solution on that path.

We find ourselves in the same position as the opponents of Jesus if we try to deny genuine healing, wherever it occurs. We have no right to dismiss techniques such as hypnosis and acupuncture as inherently evil, as I have heard some Christians do. But nor can we give blanket approval to every quack, faith healer and holy man who claims particular powers. Perhaps we should distinguish between a healing and a mere cure. There are of course real resemblances between the fundamental experiences of many who find or develop within themselves gifts of insight or healing. John Berger's moving portrait of a country doctor contains this passage about a time of personal crisis and withdrawal which he experienced prior to a new depth in his whole practice of medicine:

> It bears some resemblance to the period of isolation and crisis which precedes in Siberian and African medicine the professional emergence of the *shaman* or the *inyanga*. The Zulus have a name for this process. The *inyanga*, they say, suffers because the spirits will give him no peace and he becomes a 'house of dreams'.[20]

Suffering, ritual death and rebirth are common themes in the critical time of preparation undergone by the *shaman*, witchdoctor or sorcerer. In Scandinavian mythology the god Odin is represented as having shamanistic powers which he had secured by hanging on a cosmic tree in great suffering for nine days and nights. Despite the resemblances to the crucifixion of Jesus, it appears that this myth predates Christianity and in any case has no connection with redemptive suffering. Odin suffers for one thing only, so that he may acquire the secret knowledge of the magic runes and foretell destinies.[21]

In a novel of great imaginative power the psychologist Brian Bates has tried to reconstruct the training and initiation of an Anglo-Saxon sorcerer.[22] The book explores in narrative and dialogue form ancient ideas about the 'spirit-world' which make us question many of our modern assumptions. It is clear that the figure of Wat Brand, the Christian scribe who sets out to uncover the pagan mysteries and ends by becoming the sorcerer's apprentice, is intended in part to represent the naive modernist who refuses to give any credence to divination, omens and the evil eye. Brand is reproved by Wulf, the sorcerer, for his atomized view of life:

> You are labelling pieces of the world with words, then confusing your word-hoard for the totality of life. You see life as if you were viewing a room by the light of a single moving candle; then you make the error of assuming that the small areas you are seeing one at a time are separate and cannot be seen as one. Since the small areas of your life are thus seen as separate, you have to invent ways of connecting them. This is the fallacy of the ordinary person's view of life, for everything is already connected. Middle-Earth is one room, lit by a thousand candles.[23]

The sorcerer, of course, sees it as one. But the question that arises in my mind as I read is, whatever the truth of the sorcerer's perception and the reality therefore of his power, can you trust him? In one revealing passage in the book Brand asks Wulf why the people are afraid of him. Wulf answers that the people bring him gifts because 'they believe that if I were not treated properly, then I could bring great misfortune to them'. Chuckling, he agrees 'They are right.'[24] The dilemma is not new. The Scandinavian sagas indicate clearly that Odin the god-*shaman* is not to be trusted, and this may even be the direct reason for some of the Norse pagans turning to Christianity.[25] I myself have known a Pakistani student in Britain who felt he had to take frequent presents to the Muslim holy man whom he had consulted, because it would have been dangerous to incur his enmity. When Christian clergy acquire a reputation for being prepared to help people *unconditionally* with prayer and counselling, it is not surprising that Muslims, Sikhs and Hindus in Britain are often prepared to go to them in times of distress and anxiety.

It may objected that this, however interesting, really concerns only a few on the very margins of modern Western society, which is determinedly secular in temper and in practice. For most people religion has been successfully reduced to morality, and only a few residual superstitions affect a minority of the population. Muslims, Sikhs, Hindus and Buddhists will in time display the same Western secularity as is already evident among Jews. This is the conclusion of those who have charted the institutional decline of the British churches, which they regard as well-nigh irreversible:

> Any general re-conversion of post-Christian Britain would, of course, involve a reversal of the very essence of modern industrial society – and that is a possibility about as likely as the prospect, 2,000 years ago, that an insignificant Jewish cult might succeed in turning the great classical world upside down![26]

There is no space here to argue adequately the case that religion in all its forms is a far more obdurate survivor in modern Western society than those who will not lift their heads from church statistics can appreciate. Breakfast television has its resident astrologer, as does most of the popular press. Religious societies of all sorts continue to flourish in the universities. There is immense interest in yoga, meditation and other Hindu-Buddhist traditions. The pope draws crowds numbering hundreds of thousands wherever he goes in the world, including the West. The intense interest in film stars, pop stars and the British royal family is itself a kind of worship. The gods and heroes – male and female – walk again on earth, their very 'ordinariness' as reflected by press and television somehow proving the opposite to people who know they themselves are genuinely ordinary.

The question left over, the question which haunts all religion is Who or What is adequate for our worship? Who is adequate for our love and our trust? If we cannot trust the sorcerers and the people with secret knowledge of every kind; if the idols of our culture or our politics let us down and reveal themselves as all too human; if the causes we throw ourselves into – all the Conservations and the Liberations and the Abolitions – fade and leave us empty and disillusioned; what is there left which is worth worshipping? A question perhaps for middle age rather than youth, but Western society is now middle-aged, and inwardly alarmed at her loss of vitality, the confidence she once displayed with the impenetrable arrogance of the young. It seems to me that we do not stop worshipping. We either worship what is worthy of our worship or we worship idols, even ourselves. Our worship defines who we are, and what we are becoming. It seems to me that we need for our worship a God of infinite power who chooses not to threaten us with it; a God who encompasses every conceivable and actual experience of men and women, so that nothing can separate us from him, and who is yet totally beyond our control; a God who knows what it is like to be us in our cruel limitations and yet does not make excuses for us; a God who has gone to the uttermost limit for us but is in no way diminished or damaged by the journey.

Such a God I see in Jesus Christ. But I know that others too have glimpsed him, for 'every race of men. . . were to seek God, and, it might be, touch and find him; though indeed he is not far from each one of us, for in him we live and move, in him we exist'.[27] In fact Paul's own language here echoes that of the Greek poets long before Christ, and he goes on to quote one of them directly in the next verse: 'We are all his children.' But we dare not leave Paul's speech to the Athenians there, for that would imply that the mere attempt to reach out and find God is enough. Paul actually ended his speech with his listeners mocking him as he spoke about the judgement of God and the resurrection of Jesus. We cannot assume from the Bible, whether Old or New Testament, that provided we make some effort to worship God all will be well. There is too much prophetic denunciation of false worship for that. Idolatry creeps into all our prayers and prostrations.

Nevertheless I cannot deny the depth of devotion of people of other faiths, and if I have spent too long discussing the 'folk religion' of Islam and the animistic world it is because it has so many parallels in popular Christian and secular practice. I do not at all discount the piety of generations of Jews, Muslims, Sikhs and Hindus, or the unaffected greeting in the name of God which is common in many African languages.[28] Asking the conventional question 'How are you?' in Urdu, I often felt rebuked by the answer 'I am well – with your prayers.' Both Jew and Muslim invoke the peace of God on the most casual meeting, and whereas the 'Shalom' or 'Salaamu aleikum' may be no more consciously devotional than the English 'Goodbye' (originally 'God be with you'), there is a rich theology behind it waiting for the speaker to pause and reflect on.

These few reminders have not, of course, dealt with formal worship itself, and whether people of different faiths can ever properly come together in common worship. They merely set the scene of a common divine dimension to our lives, but that is a perspective vital to retain if we are not to be united by our godlessness. In schools in particular there is a tremendous need for the imaginative presentation of story, parable and myth, music and dance, and shared silence, as a way of preparing children for adult worship.[29] Formal adult multi-faith worship itself is a different matter. It is in normal circumstances made inappropriate by the very different claims about matters of truth – matters at the very heart of many faiths – which may form the very focus of worship itself in a particular tradition. For example, Christian worship celebrating the death and resurrection of Jesus would be quite impossible for Jews and Muslims to join, since they deny, in different ways, the reality or significance of both. Only by temporarily setting aside the specific 'jealousies' – as they have been called – of each faith, can any common worship be possible, and even then there are grave problems about language, place and posture, dress and the whole style and character of the 'service'. Very often such occasions are a wholesale capitulation to a Christian style of doing things, even in a Christian building, with very little Christian content. There are times, however, when the participants are well known to each other, when no one need feel compromised by the reading of carefully selected passages of scripture and the invitation to pray as each one can for the people or causes in mind.

What more in the end can we say about true worship than was written by the Persian poet Rumi? God is speaking:

Was it not I that summoned thee to service?
Did I not make thee busy with my name?

Thy calling 'Allah!' *was* my 'Here am I',
Thy yearning pain my messenger to thee.
Of all those tears and cries and supplications
I was the magnet, and I gave them wings.[30]

Chapter Three

FOOD

Allah's messenger said: 'Eat together, and do not separate, for the blessing is in the company.'

One of my memories of Pakistan is sitting with my Urdu teacher out of doors on a warm February morning with the smell of spices being prepared over the garden wall, so that I could hardly concentrate for the watering of my mouth. Another memory is the parties of tea and cakes and bottled drinks we were sometimes invited to by very poor people who really could not afford such extravagance but insisted on being open-handed hosts. It was a way of expressing affection but it also suggested that the honour they were paying us was theirs first, that people who treated their guests with a proper generosity had a certain nobility about them. We were constantly surprised and somewhat shamed by Eastern traditions of hospitality. I once admired a very elaborate and expensive wallhanging in someone's home, and was slightly puzzled at the off-hand reaction to my praise of it. Then I remembered that sometimes an Eastern host feels obliged to make a gift of anything a guest obviously admires, so I hastily changed the subject.

Food and hospitality are good subjects for a book on a mixed society, for food and drink lubricate meeting, and turn acquaintances into friends. But food and drink can also be an unexpected barrier, for most of the world has conventions about what you can and cannot consume, and even with whom you may consume it. The Western would-be host who invites his Asian neighbours in at Christmas time for 'mince-pies and a glass of something' may receive an embarrassed refusal, and give up trying to be friendly on the spot. Yet a little information could save him, or her, from unknowingly putting their neighbours in a very awkward situation. Mince pies are likely to be made with lard, which Muslims cannot take, and beef suet, which cuts out Hindus too. Alcohol is forbidden to Muslims and usually frowned on by Hindus and

Sikhs. Rather than accept an invitation which, however kindly meant, is going to involve a hundred and one problems of refusal and explanation and perhaps expose them as oddities, some will prefer to make their excuses and not go.

The only way round this social wall is for Westerners to begin to learn why people of certain faiths have scruples about eating some foods, and roughly which they are. For us religion is primarily a matter of thinking and feeling, and believing that certain things are so, but most of the rest of the world would find this a strange way of looking at things. For them religion is not a matter of *thinking* so much as of *doing*. For them you worship God with your stomach as well as on your knees, in your kitchen as well as in the place of prayer. Alan Unterman says of fellow-Jews: 'For the Orthodox Jew eating is a ritual activity charged with religious meaning, to be preceded and followed by the appropriate benedictions . . . part of the attempt to sanctify the ordinary life of man, and to transmute him into a holy creature of God.'[1] It may be that Jews have taken this understanding of food further than anyone else, but in many faiths the human body is sacred and therefore it matters a great deal what goes into it. The words of Jesus are much more revolutionary than Westerners normally realize:

> Do you not see that nothing that goes from outside into a man can defile him, because it does not enter his heart but into his stomach, and so passes out into the drain? Thus (comments Mark) he declared all foods clean.[2]

But for many believers, all foods are by no means clean. Many people realize that Jews and Muslims eat nothing from the pig, and Hindus will not touch beef; that Muslims are forbidden alcohol and Sikhs tobacco and alcohol. But it actually goes much further than that. The most complex and extensive food laws are to be found among the Jews, though it must be said at once that the degrees of observance vary very greatly. Lionel Blue is a Jewish rabbi of the Reform tradition who has written a cookery book (with June Rose). In it he warns that if you want to invite Jews to a meal

> For very very traditional Jews ('Torah true') the laws affecting pots, pans, cooks and food are so complex that they would probably prefer you to visit them rather than the other way round.[3]

For the rest he advises that if you keep off meat you will avoid most of the problems, though it is not always so easy to know, or remember, just what kind of animal fat is used in shop-made biscuits or cakes. With fish too, shell-fish are as forbidden as pork, and so are wriggling things like eels. The best thing of course is to ask your guests in advance what they can and cannot eat, and show interest rather than incredulity when they tell you. Most will be delighted that you should ask.

The full range of Jewish law on the subject of food is far beyond the range of a few pages in a book of this sort, but it is worth making an effort to understand something of their scope. According to Leviticus 11 and Deuteronomy 14 land animals which chewed the cud and had divided hooves were good for food. This eliminated (specifically) camels, badgers, rabbits and pigs. Any fish with fins and scales was all right, but this cut out shell-fish and eels. Birds of prey were forbidden, and so were insects (except for locusts and grasshoppers), as were moles, rats, mice and lizards. This is fairly straightforward (though a number of European delicacies have already gone!), but complications set in with the interpretation of the command: 'Do not cook a young sheep or goat in its mother's milk.'[4] This has been understood as a prohibition of mixing meat and milk dishes in the same meal, so that cheese, white coffee and most ice-creams cannot be eaten after a meat dish. Moreover in most Jewish kitchens the same pots and pans and plates are never used for both meat and milk dishes, but kept strictly separate.

If this seems bewildering, the secret lies in the sense of sanctity about a Jewish home. Lionel Blue reminisces about his grandmother's kitchen in the East End of London:

> You must realize that it was a chapel and a vestry. She processed, there is no other word for it, to the living room table which was our altar. And this is not the language of whimsy but the language of Jewish theology. For on the table among the pickles and herrings, were the great silver cup of wine, the bread waiting to be blessed, and the candles for the sanctification of the Sabbath – all the things a Christian finds when he goes to church.[5]

'The language of Jewish theology', says Blue. The *Sayings of the Fathers*, an ancient Jewish text, confirms this view.

Rabbi Simeon said, If three have eaten at a table and have spoken there no words of Torah, it is as if they had eaten of sacrifices to dead idols, of whom it is said, For all their tables are full of vomit and filthiness; the All-present is not (in their thoughts). But if three have eaten at a table and have spoken there words of Torah, it is as if they had eaten at the table of the All-present, to which the Scripture may be applied, And he said unto me, This is the table that is before the Lord.[6]

For the Jew the family table is the family altar. It follows that food offered there must be as pure as what was once offered to God in the temple at Jerusalem, it must be *kosher* (or *kāsher*), ritually clean. This means that animals and birds (but not fish) which are to serve as food must be slaughtered by an adult male Jew who pronounces the benediction over them. The Talmud gives very precise instructions as to the exact method of slaughter, which is designed to spare the animal as much pain as possible. Close inspection is made, especially of the lungs, to ensure that no disease is present in the carcase, and of course no animal which has died of natural causes can be considered for food. No fat is allowed[7] and the sciatic nerve is excised.[8] This means in practice that the major arteries are removed and the hindquarters of the animal are not used. Its blood is also removed by a lengthy salting process,[9] and this of course makes *kosher* meat more expensive than other varieties. It also means that some intestines such as liver are unusable. But is avoiding rump steak or black pudding a high price to pay for the reminder that when we eat meat we take life, and all life belongs to God? In the modern city few people have ever even slaughtered their own chickens, and it is easy to forget just what our diet involves.

Even when Jews do not observe the minutiae of the Talmudic regulations, and are prepared to eat some food prepared by non-Jews, and drink non-Jewish wine, the sense of food as an expression of religious faith persists. Sabbath and Passover, New Year and Harvest have their appropriate dishes, and the 'salt-beef Jew' is the one who only remembers the tastes of childhood, and no longer observes the faith. But he does remember, and the gastronomic calendar may recall him eventually to the events it celebrates. For many Christians the Eucharist has in recent years become a much more central act of worship than it used to be, and much more recognizable as a meal, where God's people gather to be fed by him round his table. Ordinary bread is often used in place of wafers, and the service is often celebrated in the homes of the congregation, where the armchairs and the glass of wine and the loaf of bread can recall the reality of the Last Supper more powerfully than organs and microphones and traditional vestments. And when the *seder*, or Passover meal, is led by a Jewish Christian, and its relation to the Eucharist explained in detail, Christians see more profoundly how food can become the meeting-place of God and man.

It is probably true to say that for Muslims the meeting-place of God and man is remembered by the absence of food. For the great month of fasting, Ramadhan (or Ramzān), commemorates the sending down of the Qur'an to Muhammad, and abstinence from food is meant to concentrate the mind on things of real worth.

> Eat and drink until the white thread becometh distinct to you from the black thread at the dawn. Then strictly observe the fast till nightfall and. . . be at your devotions in the mosques. . . Thus Allah expoundeth his revelations to mankind that they may ward off evil.[10]

No food or drink may pass the lips of a Muslim during the daylight hours of Ramadhan, and when the month falls in summer this calls for considerable self-discipline. (As Muslims follow a lunar calendar their year begins ten days earlier in each of ours.) In Muslim countries cafés and restaurants are only open for the use of foreigners during these days, and no food is consumed in public by anyone. When a whole community is engaged in this way, even the irreligious are caught up to some extent by its spirit, and young children plead that they are now old enough to observe the fast. In the last hour of day a stillness settles over the city, and as the light begins to fail men hurry home to break the fast with their families. A drumbeat from the mosque announces the actual ending of daylight and prayers follow immediately. When the month ends the great feast of Eid-ul-Fitr expresses the thankfulness of the whole community for another achievement of self-control exercised in obedience to God's command. But the emphasis is on God's kindness, not on self-mortification:

> Allah desireth for you ease; He desireth not hardship for
> you; and He desireth that you should complete the period,
> and that ye should magnify Allah for having guided you,
> and that peradventure ye may be thankful.[11]

The same thought governs the regulations about which foods
are permissible.

> 'O ye who believe, eat of the good things wherewith we have
> provided you, and render thanks to Allah; He hath forbid-
> den you only carrion and blood and swineflesh, and that
> which hath been immolated to any other than Allah.[12]

This is represented by Muslims as a considerable relaxation
from Jewish food laws, which according to the Qur'an were
intended for their punishment.[13] Camel, rabbit and hare come
off the forbidden list, but alcohol goes on it, closely associated
with gambling:

> They question thee (Muhammad) about strong drink and
> games of chance. Say: in both is great sin, and some utility
> for men; but the sin of them is greater than their usefulness.[14]

Animals for meat should be slaughtered in a way very similar
to the Jewish – in fact *kosher* meat is quite acceptable to
Muslims. They themselves use the term *halāl*, which means
'permitted' (as distinct from *harām*, 'unlawful'). Every part of
the pig is *harām*, and so is any meat not ritually slaughtered.
As with Jews, the degree of observance varies with individual
Muslims, but many will avoid even such apparently in-
nocuous things as bread and ice-cream, in case they contain
lard. This can cause great difficulties for Muslims, who have
not had so long to organize themselves in the West as Jews
have, and *The Muslim Guide* understandably complains:

> A Muslim has to read the list of ingredients very carefully
> whenever he intends to buy any food in the market, but
> unfortunately in Britain giving information about ingre-
> dients is not legally binding as it is in the U.S. and on the
> continent. This restriction will take even some breads, ice
> creams, biscuits and soups outside the list of what Muslims
> can eat in Britain.[15]

Again the right thing to do when inviting a Muslim to eat in
your house is to ask him what he may eat. It would obviously
be simpler to avoid meat, and considerate not to use alcohol in

front of him.

One evident result of Jewish and Muslim food-laws is to set them apart from the general population, to make their religious affiliation something constantly noticed by others, unless of course they abandon or drastically modify their observance. It also creates a situation in which Jews and Muslims prefer to live in their own areas and buy at Jewish or Muslim shops, to avoid the constant inspection of ingredients and wondering whether such and such an item is permitted. For Muslims in particular it generates the feeling that a Muslim country is a purer and a cleaner place for the absence of pork and alcohol. Added to his unease about our sexual customs this may make it profoundly difficult for a Muslim to feel really at home in the West, even if he and his family experience no kind of racial discrimination, which is – sadly – very unlikely. If he is reluctant to accept non-Muslim hospitality because of food-laws he may never see the inside of a non-Muslim home, yet he senses how difficult it may be to preserve his religious integrity while being part of Western society. The Jews, it may be claimed, have done it, but the fact is that many Jews see assimilation as a great threat to their survival as a people, perhaps as great as the persecutions of the past. The growing enthusiasm for a vegetarian diet will solve a number of problems here, as will the more precise labelling of ingredients on packaged food.

Jewish and Muslim scruples, even when we do not share them, ought to make us more alert to the way our food comes to us, to look a little more closely at our supermarket chops and mince, and at the life they once shared with us. Among Hindus that life is thought to be shared much more extensively. The idea of reincarnation involves a succession of births, some of which may be in animal form. To kill an animal therefore is to bring to an end one incarnation of the soul and precipitate another. Many Hindus in consequence prefer to eat no meat at all, and in particular no beef, since the cow is venerated as the symbol and source of all fertility. Each caste has its own particular rules for what may be eaten, and the higher the caste the more stringent the regulations, so that Brahmins may avoid even fish and onions, which are thought to stimulate sexual feelings. Among Hindus, however, the question that is often more important than what you eat is who cooks it and with whom you eat it. Caste restrictions are now greatly relaxed compared with the days when Gandhi had to go through a ceremony of puriication after his return from studying in Britain, because of the pollution he incurred by doing so. Nevertheless in many Indian village weddings today the castes sit separately, though invited to the same feast, and the cooks are always Brahmins, since everyone can take food from them without fear of ritual pollution. In Britain Brahmins run businesses involving the preparation of food for the same reason, the local caste societies tend to preserve the custom of eating only with members of one's own caste.[16]

Such caste loyalites have been vigorously rejected by Buddhists and in particular by Sikhs. Buddhists prohibit alcohol, and will not kill animals for food, but otherwise have no dietarty restrictions. Sikhs forbid alcohol and tobacco and other intoxicants, but the only other dietary law is said to be that of eating food which is earned honestly. Sikhs characteristically reject the rituals observed by other faith communities, and a telling command is:

As beef is to the Hindu and pork to the Muslim so other people's property should be to a Sikh.[17]

It much be in consequence of the opposition to ritual ('Rituals and ceremonies are chains of the mind') that an initiated (Khalsa) Sikh is *forbidden* to eat meat killed by the Muslim method of ritual slaughter – surely a unique stand against the scruples of another faith. It may stem from the bloody encounters of Sikhs and Muslims in the seventeenth century. The Sikh scriptures firmly reject the idea of ritual pollution, and in consequence the difficulties of caste inter-dining, and the idea that eating meat is polluting. Many Sikhs however do observe the Hindu practice of vegetarianism, and in the gurdwara (Sikh temple) no meat is served and no visitor embarrassed. This seems faithful to Guru Nanak's words: 'Fools quarrel over flesh, but they do not know God and do not meditate upon him.'[18]

The Sikh practice of the *langar* or 'holy kitchen' deserves some study. The *langar* appears to date back to Guru Nanak, the founder of Sikhism (1469–1539), in his struggle against caste attitudes among his followers, but it was the third Guru,

Amar Das (1479–1574), who emphasized it as a means of unity and equality. A famous story tells of the great Mughal Emperor Akbar visiting Guru Amar Das at his village, when instead of being met by the Sikh leader he was asked to sit on the ground with other visitors and share a simple meal. It was pointed out that the Guru's rule was 'first eat together, then meet together', and Akbar, to his credit, complied. High or low, rich or poor, Hindu or Muslim, all had to share food together in the presence of the Guru. Today the *langar* takes place after the main service in the gurdwara, and though men and women sit separately, everyone takes a turn in the preparation of food. And the food is for every member of the congregation and whatever visitors there may be, of any faith or none. It is both humbling and inspiring to be served a simple but delicious meal in the hall adjoining the prayer-room, and to realize that in many Sikh gurdwaras this happens almost every evening, entirely at the expense of the faithful. No visitor is made to feel an outsider, for the very purpose of the *langer* is to bind people together in the service of the one God and in his presence to forget distinctions of race and class. It cannot be said that caste feelings and practice find no place among Sikhs but the constant intention is to overcome this and every other source of divisiveness. Something of the spirit of Sikhism may be seen in the Ninth Guru, Tegh Bahadur ('Sword of Courage'), who earnt his name in battles against the Mughal forces, but who preferred to call himself Degh Bahadur ('Cooking-pot of Courage'), since he wanted to be known as one who fed the hungry rather than as one who killed his enemies.[19]

The Sikh tradition of hospitality takes us back to our starting-point in Eastern custom. It is beautifully expressed in John Carden's series of meditations on Pakistani life:

Noon. Loitering, easily diverted, three children make their way to their village home. The scene is typical of that outside a thousand Punjabi villages about this time of the day. The demands of an empty stomach lead to the same dull meal of leathery bread and lentils with perhaps a little vegetable and chillies, over-cooked. Preference is given to the men and to any relative or visitor who may happen to call.

At first, inevitably, the children grumble among themselves about this, particularly when there is little left for them, or when some visitor makes a habit of called at food time. This state of affairs continues until their mother has a chance to do what successive generations of Punjabi mothers have done, and gathers her children round her.

'Bachay, children,' she says. 'We Punjabi people, though poor, have always believed that we must welcome an unexpected guest arriving at our door. Even though he comes empty-handed, and even though there is little in the house, we should always have eyes to see that balanced on his head he carries a pot, containing God's gift towards our daily needs.'

From their very earliest days then, this figure of God's invisible gift, unfailingly accompanying each visitor, is taken into people's lives. It prompts a sense of hospitality, and willingness to share their food with all who come, and makes kings and queens of little ragged under-fed children such as are making their way home all over Pakistan at noon today.[20]

Christians may remember the command: 'Remember to welcome strangers in your homes. There were some who did that and welcomed angels without knowing it.'[21] This verse itself recalls the visit to Abraham of the three angles who came to announce the birth of Isaac.[22]

The meaning of hospitality goes much further than the offering of food. To sit down and eat together is an ancient symbol of friendship and good will, and among religious people has always indicated a common share in God's goodness, and a determination to remember in thankfulness what he has done in giving and preserving our lives. It is a sad thing when religious scruples prevent people from sitting down to eat together, especially when, as so often in Western societies, those most affected are discriminated against in other ways. If those of us who are white Anglo-Saxons, or in other ways part of the majority, are going to call ourselves the 'host community', we ought at least to see that our 'guests' are able to feel at ease in our homes. This may mean that all we can offer the strictly orthodox Jew or Brahmin is fresh fruit which he can peel himself, but we can at least offer that (preferably on a new disposable plate!). And with the offer genuinely and seriously made, we can leave the interpretation of his food-laws to him. As Lionel Blue says: 'You may be your brother's keeper but you're not his nanny.'[23]

The tragedy is that most ethnic minorities in Western countries are well aware that 'host' and 'guest' is a very misleading way of describing the situation which they face. The Turkish and other migrant workers in West Germany have been called *gastarbeiter* – 'guest-workers' – but they know that they are even less welcome guests during an economic recession than they were before. In other countries Hindus, Sikhs and Muslims find their legal position more favourable, while the earlier generation of Jewish migrants are perma-nently settled. Nevertheless even people long settled can be made to feel profoundly unsettled, when their customs and perhaps their colour mark them out as different from the majority. The offer and sharing of food can be one way to bridge the gap, even if it requires some adjustment from those who have no food-laws to observe.

Nor are the advantages all one way. As we have seen, the customs of others can compel us to re-examine our own, and in this case to recall in particular what is involved in eating meat, that is the life of an animal. The fact that we have no religious scruples about food need not make us careless about what we eat. Our present prodigal use of natural resources involves immense amounts of grain being fed to animals bred for slaughter, while others starve for lack of just that grain. A little thought may make us ask whether a much more res-trained use of meat might not benefit the entire world. Already we are being made more conscious of the cost in human terms of many of our imports, of tea, coffee and sugar, and it is a serious question for some whether to buy fruit from South Africa. When Jesus 'declared all foods clean'[24] he surely did not mean us to stop thinking about where it came from, or how it arrived on our plates. He merely meant that no food is unclean of itself, but it is the way that we obtain it and our attitude towards it which makes us clean or unclean.

Chapter Four

Sex and Gender

On one occasion in the university in Pakistan I was introduced to a member of the library staff, a Muslim lady. In British fashion I stuck out my hand, and when she appeared reluctant to take it, persevered in the expectation that she would adjust to my custom. But her Muslim reserve was stronger than my boldness, and I ruefully lowered my hand as she said, 'Men and women don't shake hands with each other in this country.' I had been wrong, of course, to persist in trying to make her meet me in my fashion, but the incident is a trivial reminder of the vastly different relationships which men and women have with one another in different cultures, and the way that such behaviour patterns are often powerfully reinforced by religious feeling even when they do not clearly originate from religious law.

Islam is the subject of much strong feeling on this subject, and many Westerners find their liberal sympathies severely strained when it comes to the Muslim 'attitude to women'. It must be remembered, however, that some 50 per cent of all Muslims *are* women, and many of them share the attitudes of male spokesmen on Islam towards the proper role of men and women in society. One of the surprises of the Iranian Revolution has been the willingness of women educated in the West, sometimes at universities in California, to return to the *chadar* (veil) and the traditional custom of separating women from unrelated men.

The social anthropologist Patricia Jeffery encountered a different outlook, however, among those women whose husbands were involved in the administration of a famous Muslim shrine in North India. The reputation of the shrine, and the nature of their husbands' work, demanded an exemplary standard of conduct from the families employed there, and the women described their consequent way of life as that of frogs at the bottom of a well. They were conscious that there was a world outside the well, but they could see only that small patch of sky immediately over their heads. There was

not the remotest possibility of leaving the place where they
were. Patrica Jeffery describes her own reactions to their
situation, and her struggle to make some of the men realize
that in spite of being a woman she was intelligent enough to
understand the workings of the shrine, and was interested
enough to inquire seriously about it. Significantly, she had no
difficulty in convincing the women of her seriousness, but

> I had to contend with my own confused and ambivalent
> response to the seclusion of the women who became my
> friends. . . I could not enjoy watching the trauma which
> even crossing the road on their own caused some of them. I
> could scarcely smile at their laughter over getting lost or
> even misdirected through their ignorance of their own city.
> How could I approve of a system which creates women who
> are so 'ashamed' that they rarely leave their homes during
> daylight (even though their double veil completely conceals
> their facial features), or who always peep cautiously outside
> to check that there are no men in the alley before they set
> foot outside their homes? At the same time, how could I fail
> to be cheered by the various ploys which women made use
> of to evade the system or cover up for one another?[1]

I am reminded of the message of much of Solzhenitsyn's
writing, especially *A Day in the Life of Ivan Denisovich*, that even
in the harshest and most circumscribed situations, humanity
and humour have a way of breaking through, and men and
women learn the trick of distancing themselves from their
misfortunes and refusing to be dragged down by them. Pity by
itself is an inadequate response to such strict *pardah* (literally
'curtain', and so the custom of secluding women from public
[male] view), for it fails to recognize the achievement of
women in making the system, to some extent, serve them.
Similarly non-Muslim men cannot know, and few nonMuslim
women are admitted to any experience of the dominant
position a Muslim mother can exercise behind the scenes in
her own home. Controlling the family budget, having the
decisive voice in the schooling, upbringing and marriages of
her children, even determining the details of her daughter-in-
law's and grandchildrens' lives, the Muslim mater familias is
frequently a most powerful, though generally invisible, presence in the Muslim community.

But that invisibility, of course, debars her from public life, and although there have been, and are, significant women in public life in Muslim countries – Fatima Jinnah, Begum Nusrat Bhutto and her daughter Benazir are immediate examples from Pakistan – such women do not keep the traditional status of *pardah*. They have generally won their public position through being associated with a male relative who had previously been politically eminent. Such women often see themselves as continuing their husband's or father's or brother's work. A Muslim Mrs Thatcher, achieving power through her own gifts alone, is almost inconceivable.

The twin reasons for this are that marriage is expected of every Muslim, and once married, the Muslim woman's primary responsibilities are to be within the home. 'The husband's major responsibility', says *The Muslim Guide*, 'is that of earning all the economic and material needs of the family, thus, in effect, fulfilling his wife's clearly defined right to this provision, without being in any way compelled to contribute financially herself, however independently wealthy she may be.'[2] The Muslim woman, it asserts, is in no way to be thought spiritually or intellectually inferior to her brother, and nothing should stand in the way of the development of her full potential. The *Guide* declares, somewhat defensively, that 'there is no significant evidence to indicate that Muslim parents in Britain attach more importance to the education of their sons rather than their daughters and to both they appear to give equal freedom of choice in careers, with due regard to the equally important but essentially different primary role they will play in adult life.'[3] Nevertheless many Muslim girls are reported to have waged long battles with their parents before they were allowed to take up a place in college.

However, it does need to be recognized that where there is strong opposition to a daughter's college career from Muslim parents it is not any opposition to education as such, but the open society of student life, and the dangers and temptations they feel sure their daughter will be exposed to there. The traditional Muslim girl has been encouraged to develop her understanding of the Qur'an, and it is well known that the first teachers of Islam to children are invariably their mothers. It is the mothers too who, as in other faiths, set the example to the rest of the family in the observance of ritual prayer and the annual fast. Learning itself presents no problem. 'Seek knowledge, though it be in China' the prophet is reported to have said. But the context of student freedom as traditionally understood in the West makes many Muslim families fear for the reputation and moral safety of their daughters.

The daughter is the bearer of the family honour in much of Asian society. Not only for Muslims, but for Hindus and Sikhs too, a daughter may be an economic liability because of the cost of getting her married, and she will be unable to provide the security a son can afford for his parents' old age. In spite of this, or perhaps because of it, she is honoured as the pure, chaste virgin, the flower of her father's household. Western feminists will probably view with cynicism the double standard implied here, and there is no doubt that the reputation of a girl's moral character, and the fear of losing it, sometimes governs her life to a degree which Westerners would find quite intolerable. For an older girl in particular imprudent behaviour can affect not only her own chances of a 'good' marriage, but those of her unmarried brothers and sisters as well. We shall consider marriage further in the next chapter. Here the point is that for Asians sexual activity for women before marriage leads to deep family distress, and much of the circumstances of a girl's life will be shaped to prevent it. Men are in theory equally obliged to be sexually pure, but practical concern is overwhelmingly for the girls.

It can easily be imagined how Western society, in its public display of affection between the sexes, in its advertisements and films, and in its contemporary tolerance towards sexual activity before and outside of marriage, affronts many Asian newcomers in the most sensitive and cherished area of their lives. It is not that they are 'prudish' while Westerners are 'permissive', though that is the common stereotype. Most Westerners would regard it as extremely indelicate to make a public exhibition of the sheet from the nuptial bed with its blood-stain 'proving' the bride's pre-marital virginity. Yet that has been the immemorial custom of many Muslim families in Egypt.

There is of course a 'double standard' operating to the advantage of promiscuous males, and the doctor and novelist Nawal El Saadawi, once Egypt's Director of Public Health, has vigorously exposed the hypocrisy of her fellow-countrymen's sexual manners in her book *The Hidden Face of Eve*. Her long experience as the counsellor of many unhappy young girls convinced her that 'a segregated society with strict separation between the sexes creates widespread sexual frustration and suppression'. She describes the girls from rural poverty who become domestic servants in the houses of middle and upper class urban families:

> These girls become the only sexual object available to the young males, and sometimes even the elder males, in the family. The adolescent boys find them much more suitable to their needs than a sister, cousin or female student at school or in college. The boys are less liable to feel guilty if sex is practised with a servant girl, and in addition they are not doing wrong to somebody of their own class, but to a creature who is socially very much their inferior.[4]

Western readers of Nawal El Saadawi are reminded of conditions in Western societies before the widespread availability of contraception, and may well conclude that their own society is not in fact more immoral than either their past or the Asian present, but simply more open and (for good or ill) less easily persuaded of guilt in sexual matters. We shall come to the effect of this situation on divorce in the next chapter. Here it is important to review Saadawi's claim at the end of her book that

> Islamic, Arab or Eastern cultures are not exceptional in having transformed woman into a commodity or a slave. Western culture and Christianity have subjected women to exactly the same fate. As a matter of fact, the oppression of woman exercised by the Christian Church and those who upheld its teachings has been even more ferocious.[5]

Egyptian Muslims, despite the large Coptic church in their midst, are not normally in any way familiar with Christian doctrine or history, and Saadawi's remarks about Christianity indicate no more than a widespread Muslim presumption that Western culture and Christianity are more or less identical. It is far beyond the scope of this book to investigate the comparative history of the treatment of women in different societies. But a Christian feels compelled to point out to those who agree with Nawal El Saadawi about the church's record that the New Testament gives clear evidence of the unusual respect and consideration with which Jesus treated the women whom he met. Many of them became his followers and supported Jesus and the twelve disciples financially. Women were the first witnesses of the resurrection and were represented among local leaders in the early church. In the second century the North African Tertullian spoke of the amazing qualities of Christian women, and how important was their influence on their pagan husbands. Some of the church's early theologians succumbed to anti-women prejudice which may have originated from Manicheean sources, but others pioneered female monastic communities and the beginnings of female education.

The fact is that in days of chronic warfare society was invariably organized by its male warriors, and the status of women was inevitably dependent on their menfolk's disposition. This is reflected in virtually all religious literature. Ritual practice has often insisted on the segregation of sexes at the time of prayer. Not only Muslims but Orthodox Jews and Christians in many parts of the world today seat the sexes separately when it comes to worship. Typically, religious leaders of every faith are male, and there has been a strong feeling in the patriarchal cultures shaped by Judaism, Christianity and Islam that a female priest or priestess is somehow associated with witchcraft and the occult, or even that impeccably orthodox prayer led by a woman is somehow inauthentic. Worshippers in these scriptural faiths clung to male dominance in religious affairs perhaps because exclusively maleled worship best expressed rejection of the overt sexuality of the divinities worshipped in classical Greece and Rome and in the Arabian peninsula.

Such historic prejudice does not of course argue the continuation of a ban on women as religious leaders today, and a growing number of women are now taking their place as Christian ministers and Jewish rabbis. These movements are both in the Reformed traditions, it is true, rather than in more conservative circles, and in the Muslim world not at all.

Outside the Semitic, scriptural tradition which marks Judaism, Christianity and Islam the place of sexuality in religion is rather different. Nothing in what follows should be taken to imply that people of Eastern religious traditions are less or more observant of sexual morality than people of the Semitic traditions and cultures. But it is difficult to deny that the place of the *lingam* (male organ) in the tradition of Hindu worship centred on Shiva does actually represent a different understanding of sexuality and its significance, particularly its suitability to suggest images used in worship. The *lingam* is usually represented – often in a highly stylized way – fixed in the *yoni* (female organ), and it is said that this conveys the idea of the unity of deity and humanity in a powerful, universal image. Clearly sexual union is a theme which runs through much religious imagery all over the world, appearing in the biblical *Song of Songs* and mystical poetry of every kind, including that of Islam. But the significance of erotic imagery in Hinduism, in the cults both of Krishna and of Shiva, seem to be more than an explicit celebration of human love in a religious context. It is bound up with the question of power.

The issue may be understood by an explanation of the traditional myths about Shiva. For in Shiva the erotic and the ascetic meet, creating a paradox which has been said to lie at the very heart of Hinduism.[6] Zaehner describes the sculptures and other representations of Shiva as showing him 'permanently ithyphallic (sexually aroused) yet perpetually chaste: how is one to explain such a phenomenon?'[7] The answer of course lies partly in the nature of myth, which abounds in contradictory states and every kind of superhuman feature such as the third eye, and the ability to change one's appearance altogether. Myths enable people to consider possibilities which are not part of normal life – in this case the joys of sexual union, and the austerity of a life devoted to prayer and meditation, combined in the same being at the same time. But in addition to this there is a fundamental belief which runs through much of Hinduism and is seen also in certain forms of Buddhism and Taoism: that the spending of sexual energy, in particular the emission of semen, represents a serious loss to oneself and the world as a whole. Because sex is bound up with creativity, sexual energy is a form of power, spiritual power. One way therefore of acquiring power is to amass sexual energy by 'sustained continence,' spending time in fasting and prayer. In the myths about Shiva the god does this until the other gods become fearful of the result of so much *tapas* ('austerity', and therefore power), and beg him to discontinue it. He does so, but only to begin making love to his wife, Parvati. His *tapas* has built up such stores of energy that the couple is able to continue love-play apparently indefinitely, thus generating dangerous heat but coming to no consummation. (This kind of intercourse is sometimes known as 'coitus reservatus'). Again the gods become alarmed at this display of energy, and worried that it will not produce the son that they need, and that even if it does a son produced by such prodigious love-play will prove to be a danger to the universe.[8]

Hindu mythology, like others of ancient times, is full of explicit stories of the sexual exploits of the gods and its literature contains detailed instructions for love-play. Most famous is the *Kama Sutra* or 'Verses of Desire'. There is a marked tendency in modern times to 'spiritualize' this element in the religion, and to see in erotic sculpture, for example, the infinite varieties of *yoga* (union) between the divine essence and the human seeker. But others view this aspect of Hinduism as part of its candid worldliness and declare, as Nirad Chaudhuri does, that Hinduism is fundamentally an encyclopaedia of ways to worldly success, of how to order the universe to your own advantage.

> Hinduism differs fundamentally from Christianity in this, that for its followers it is not an alternative to the world, but primarily the means of supporting and improving their existence in it. . . . Salvation is never the object of the religious observances and worship of the Hindus. The main object is worldly prosperity. . .[9]

Chaudhuri may be more refreshing than reliable as an interpreter of Hinduism, or so Ninian Smart suggested in reviewing his book, and modern Hinduism may in any case be 'drearily Puritanical' in comparison with its ancient texts. The point here is not so much to investigate the nature of Hinduism as to note one significant understanding of sexuality within it.

If sexual energy is isolated from the total life of a loving couple, and celebrated not just as one of the principal pleasures in life but as the source of all creative power, there is a danger that the sexual element in human beings becomes sanctified as the major means of exploiting other people. Krishna's games with the *gopis*, the wives of the cowherds, are frankly adulterous, and freely described as such in the Hindu scriptures, however much modern interpreters want to promote a more 'spiritual' understanding of them. The point is made unmistakably in the *Bhagavata Purana* when certain Brahmin women come and offer themselves to Krishna. In order to test their devotion he accuses them of adulterous desires and unchaste thoughts, and they feel ashamed and withdraw, thus losing their opportunity of union with him. *Gopis*, cowherd women, also come and are tested in the same way but refuse to be shamed out of their intentions, at which Krishna rewards each of them with sexual intercourse, described in detail in the text.[10] Even Krishna's wife, Radha, has deserted her husband for him. Such desertion is actually praised as proof of the determination of the women to be united with the god, and Radha in particular is thought of as the soul passionately seeking union with the divine being, who alone holds meaning and happiness for her, whose service justifies all infidelity to lesser beings.

The Western reader, however, is bound to ask whether adulterous copulation is an appropriate image for the exalted state it is intended to represent. The question becomes even more insistent when the Tantric tradition of sex mysticism is considered, in which male and female worshippers have ritual intercourse with one another in the belief that their bodies are thereby divinized to become part of the cosmic body which is the true world. The *coitus reservatus* of the myths of Shiva also form part of this tradition, which has its Buddhist and Taoist expressions too.

I must repeat that this excursion into the Hindu tradition is not intended to suggest that Hindus are more adulterous than other people, or that prolonged study of the Hindu scriptures leads to sexual immorality. After all sex manuals are on sale in Western bookshops, and modern Western versions of the *Kama Sutra*, freely illustrated, must have made handsome profits for their publishers. The West as a whole cannot maintain any sense of superiority in sexual matters when promiscuity and its attendant venereal diseases, marital infidelity and crimes of violence against women, from wife-battering to rape, are all on the increase. But if we are to recover, or find, a proper understanding for the sexual element of our human nature, male and female, we are bound to examine what various religious traditions have to offer.

A strong Hindu tradition represents sexuality as *creative* energy. Obviously there are good reasons for this. But it does not represent sexuality as *created* energy, for doctrines of creation, though present in Hinduism, are not an integral part of it. There is no sense in which human beings are responsible, as trustees, for the powers created within them and the uses to which they are put. In Western society, with its catastrophic record of marital breakdown in recent years, we can see how the absence of any notion of responsibility *to* a Creator *for* our treatment of one another may blind us to any good but what we imagine to be our own. So we are abandoned to be victims of our own perpetually shifting inclinations, unable to say No because there seems to be no proper reason left for self-denial. Where the powerful sexual drive is concerned the result is a trail of disaster. In traditional Hindu society, as among all conservative peoples, disaster is held at bay by a series of laws, the breaking of which lead to punishment in a future existence if not in this one. But some Westerners seem to have adopted the Hindu view of sexuality as power, and to be pursuing a sex-mysticism of their own which scorns all law and all taboo. With the fear of unwanted pregnancy removed by contraceptive devices even incest and sexual interference with children has been openly advocated, and the latter commercially exploited in pornography.

A recent case in Britain brought to trial a woman who had been goaded beyond endurance by years of beatings from her husband. He had forced her into prostitution and constantly abused her. Her face bore permanent evidence of his cruelty. One fateful night she poured paraffin over him and struck a match. He died from 90 per cent burns. In the face of such appalling misery it is difficult to repeat with confidence that humanity is made in the image of God. Yet Judaism and Christianity not only acknowledge that responsible trusteeship from the Creator, mentioned above, which Islam also knows, but actually sees men and women as being like God.

'So God created human beings making them to be like himself. He created them male and female.'[11] So made, they were meant, in the biblical understanding, to embody in themselves the love and goodness of God towards one another. Like him they were to be creative, filling his world with new evidence of his imaginative power and loveliness. 'He blessed them and said, "Have many children, so that your descendants will live all over the earth and bring it under their control."'[12]

Traditionally commentators have made much of the fact that sexuality is only recorded in the biblical narrative after the disobedience of Adam and Eve had led to their expulsion from the Garden of Eden. I think there is no doubt we are intended to understand that sexuality, like all human capacity, is seriously impaired by the Fall of man and woman, and liable like all other aspects of human nature, to misuse. There is also the suggestion that the dominance of men is part of the punishment which has fallen on both sexes. 'And he said to the woman, "I will increase your trouble in pregnancy and your pain in giving birth. In spite of this you will still have desire for your husband, yet you will be subject to him."'[13] Before their disobedience they had no knowledge of their own nakedness, but after it they try to cover themselves with leaves. It is surely significant that God does not tell them to put away their pathetic attempts at dressmaking and return to the way they were created, but makes clothes for them out of animal skins. There is no way back to the original innocence, and in fact the animal world must now also suffer for human foolishness, since animals must die in order to provide the skins to clothe them. At their creation the intention was that the man and the woman should be creative in the manner of God, for the benefit of the entire universe. After the Fall it seems that their sexuality is a narrower and poorer thing, its expression made at the cost of the animal kingdom, and itself a source of tribulation as well as of comfort to them.

Early Christian thinkers pointed out that Jesus was called the second Adam, obedient to God where Adam had been disobedient and thus fulfilling the true purpose of God in creating man. So Mary too was obedient where Eve had been disobedient. In fact where Eve's disobedience had led to the

subsequent fall of her husband, Mary's obedience had led to
the birth of the Saviour. In both cases the decisive step was
taken by women. (The New Testament itself does not explicitly draw the second parallel, perhaps fearing to take the
analogy of Jesus and Adam too far. Jesus in Christian thought
is not merely a representative man.) The new respect and
status of women is unmistakable in the New Testament, as
noted above, even if the church did not always live up to the
originality of the gospel it had received. The apostle Paul
affirms the married state gladly (not grudgingly as many have
alleged) but also calls men and women to consider remaining
unmarried for the sake of God's kingdom. Essentially the New
Testament proclaims a restoration of the sexual factor in men
and women to the universal intention which lay behind it in
the beginning, but which had become perverted to much
narrower and more selfish ends. Paul even declares the
essential irrelevance of the notion of gender in the face of what
has happened in the coming of Christ. 'So there is no
difference between Jews and Gentiles, between slaves and free
men, between men and women; you are all one in union with
Christ Jesus.'[14] Of course the outward distinctions and different ways of life continue, but there is an essential inner unity
now between those who are taking part in the re-creation of
the world. 'When anyone is joined to Christ, he is a new
being.'[15]

The Western world does not recognize sexuality as a gift to
be held in trust, and used and directed for the benefit of the
whole community. It sees only a possession to be exploited for
the exclusive benefit of its possessor and his or her successive
partners. Since women were released from the fear of pregnancy by contraception this attitude, formerly more typical
of men, has spread to women also. And with it has come
endless misery. The women's movement, protesting against
male exploitation, is in danger of demanding the right for
women to be exploitive in their turn. What is needed, as many
have seen, is a new understanding of what it means to be truly
human, whether male or female. So we find ourselves asking
again what it means to be made in the image of God.

Chapter Five

Marriage and Family

Perhaps the greatest contrast between East and West today is found in the custom of arranged marriages. Westerners view almost with disbelief the willingness of many Asian boys and girls whom they know at school or college to accept the life partner chosen for them by their parents. Yet arranged marriages were at one time the universal practice of the royal families of Europe, and very prevalent among commoners too. It is said that the tradition of the French as great lovers springs from the custom of arranged marriages because of which every woman had her *amant* as well as her husband.

Romantic love is a constant feature – indeed the mainstay – of Indian and Pakistani films as it is of Western. But in the Eastern tradition the romantic love attachment is invariably ill-fated. After a brief encounter the lovers are separated by their shocked parents or by other, even crueller circumstances, and meet if at all only at the end of the film in a cloud-filled fantasy-world after the death of one or even both of them. Romantic love, the message goes, may be a profound and wonderful experience, but it is no basis for marriage. Boys and girls must be gently or sharply dissuaded from attempting to build on such a dream-world the solid realities of family life. To marry for love is a piece of foolishness from which the couple will awake to penury and unhappiness. Their parents will not support them in such a mad adventure and deprived of family wisdom and encouragement they will turn against each other. Even if they persist in such unnatural conduct the result can only be misery for everyone involved.

So runs a common enough opinion in the Indian sub-continent. Of course the path of true love does sometimes run smooth, especially when the young couple are shrewd enough to get their parents to negotiate their marriage for them. Parents who have more confidence in the maturity of their children than in their own judgement in a rapidly changing world may well feel relieved of a major responsibility if they can work according to the preferences of their children while preserving the formality of parental choice. But at other times the requirements of land or dynasty or ambitious connection may point to a marriage which in Western minds means the sacrifice of the happiness of a teenage girl on the altar of an old man's lust or loneliness. Patricia Jeffery found when trying to identify the outlying members of a family that 'it does not matter who exactly a man's wife is, as long as she comes from a good family. . . Women are continually lost from genealogical memory, they are structurally irrelevant. No line continues unless there are sons, and yet the production of sons relies on the presence of wives.'[1]

Women are lost from genealogical memory primarily because on marriage they leave their own family for that of their husband. The new couple's home is invariably that of the husband's parents or even grandparents, and the new wife learns her domestic role and sometimes many of her cooking skills from her mother-in-law. If the mother-in-law is young or sympathetic enough to recall the similar tutoring of her own mother-in-law she may prove a wise and welcome companion. But equally she may have learnt to enjoy the power that tradition gives her in this one limited area of life, and compensate for powerlessness outside the home by tyranny within it. In either case she is likely to support her son against her daughter-in-law in any possible clash. Sons are her own guarantee of acceptance and value within the family, for sons alone ensure its continuance and the economic and social well-being of the parents into old age. Parents cannot presume that a married daughter will be able to care for them then, but a son must do so. Or rather his wife will do so at his bidding. Long before that, of course, sons provide the income and status of the family while the daughters' contribution is at best adornment. As a Muslim daughter-in-law she is entitled to full control over her own wealth (see chapter 4), but may have little opportunity to spend that money on herself. Patricia Jeffery's researches were admittedly into an extreme form of female seclusion, but she reports that it was common among the Muslim women of her acquaintance not to receive the share of their father's estate to which they were entitled, for 'a woman may waive her rights, or "forgive" her brother, provided that she does so "out of happiness" and not "under pressure". If a man dies without giving his sister her due, he will suffer in the afterlife, unless she has forgiven him. But it is considered honourable for a woman to forego her rights.'[2] Similarly she may 'forgive' her husband the payment which he should make to her at the time of marriage.

Gifts of goods or money are universal in marriage customs all over the world, but in South Asia they are regarded as an integral part of the marriage arrangement itself, and not just as a natural part of the two families' love and generosity. This, together with the fact that the marriage is invariably arranged by the parents and not by the young people themselves, inevitably gives the sense of a bargain being struck, or a contract sealed. Muslim law actually does regard the marriage as a contract between the bridegroom and the father or guardian of the bride – not the girl herself. Traditionally it gives the right to the father or grandfather of either the boy or the girl to marry them even without their consent, if they are under the age of puberty. Today most Muslim countries have laws forbidding child marriages, and the consent of both parties is necessary, though, again according to Muslim law, the silence of a virgin girl is held to be her consent. The underlying assumption is that at marriage a woman passes from the care and protection of her father and brothers to the care and protection of her husband and his male relatives. As an assurance of his good faith the husband gives to her the *mahr* or marriage settlement. In pre-Islamic times this was a bride-price paid to her family. Today a part of it must normally by paid at the marriage, and the rest either at its consummation, or in instalments, or only in the case of a divorce. As noted above a wife may feel it wise not to insist on its full payment, and she will 'earn merit' by 'forgiving' him.

In addition to the marriage settlement, which is prescribed by Islamic law, the Muslims of the sub-continent have adopted the Sikh and Hindu custom of dowry (*jahēz*), which is a set of gifts given by the parents of the bride for the establishment of the new home. Since that new home will, to begin with at least, be with the husband's family, the gifts are effectively made to them. In India the custom of dowry has been forbidden by law, but still continues as one of the evils of society. Amrit Wilson found in 1978 that sums between £500 and £2,000 were quite normal for dowries among Gujerati

Hindu families in Britain. She was told by a Gujerati mother:

> Of course, not every marriage involves a dowry but among
> Patels the majority do. Some parents may give because they
> want to, that's different. But the trouble is that people like
> to copy and outdo each other and it is taken out on the girl.
> She may be asked by her parents-in-law why she hasn't
> brought a bigger dowry. And apart from the actual dowry
> there is the jewellery. There is the custom that the jewellery
> must be displayed. . . Unfortunately what it amounts to is
> pure materialism, people showing off what they have got.[3]

If a girl from a Sikh or Hindu family is allowed to take a job in
Britain she does not necessarily become more independent.
Before marriage her earnings may simply go towards her
dowry, and after it she may have to hand all her wages over to
her husband's family, and even he may have no say in the
matter.

It is easy to see that the extended family system can lead to
gross abuse and unhappiness for the young girl who joins it as
a bride, perhaps of one of the junior brothers. In her father's
house she was often called a guest, because everyone knew it
would not be long before she left. Here she may feel more like
a slave. But it would be quite wrong to suggest that extended
families and their arranged marriages cannot produce very
great happiness and both material and emotional security.
Arranged marriages begin perhaps with greater realism than
is common in the starry-eyed romantic tradition of the West.
Marriage is regarded as the beginning of love, not as the end
of a passionate courtship. Couples do grow to love each other,
perhaps with more tolerance and less disillusionment. In that
context love can be thought of realistically as a consistent
effort of the will, a determined search for the good of the other.
In the popular songs of the West, and in the gossip columns of
its newspapers, love sounds more like a disease that strikes
without reason and without mercy. It is a wind that blows
everything before it, and no one can be held responsible for its
effects, whatever unfaithfulness and desertion may result.

Divorce has always been part of Muslim, Sikh and Hindu
life, though Muslims insist that of all things lawful and not
actually forbidden, it is the thing most hateful to God.
Naturally, since two families brought about and sustained the

marriage, two families are involved in its ending, and this in itself may be enough to stimulate successful attempts at reconciling the couple. The girl's family in particular will not want to take on the difficult task of securing a second marriage for their daughter, but the boy's family may also see divorce as a slur on themselves. Here the reputation of the family, often felt to limit the freedom of its younger members, operates to sustain the stability of the family of the next generation. So the technical ease of divorce, especially in Islam, is limited in practice by the checks and balances, built in by family custom and the traditions of a whole way of life. We saw that female seclusion is alleviated by the ability of the women it confines to invent ways of overcoming it. So arranged marriages are not all that they seem to be, and the extended family is a complex social institution of great natural strength.

But we are concerned in this book with a mixed society, and the mingling of custom and culture in what is hoped will be the enrichment of a whole nation. Here the image of transplant surgery comes to mind, for it is a serious question whether the cluster of Asian family customs described above can survive more than one generation in the West. Will the graft 'take', or be decisively rejected by the host body? While the immigrant generation lives on, with its own language and newspapers and preoccupations from the original homeland, the forms at least are maintained, but signs of serious strain are already evident and as the generation born in this country reaches adulthood great changes occur.

British Jews have long been articulate about the problems of 'assimilation' for their own identity as Jewish people, and have now begun to ask whether that is not actually a greater threat to their existence as a people than the persecution of past centuries, and of the Nazi attempt to eliminate Jewry altogether. Jewish anxieties often focus on intermarriage, for having achieved the entry of their sons and daughters into universities and colleges and subsequent professional careers Jewish parents are now finding that one in three of their children (sons especially) are marrying non-Jews. Rabbi Dow Marmur reports that

The Anglo-Jewish community, indeed the Jewish Diaspora as a whole, is understandably alarmed by the threat of intermarriage. Many communal activities, especially those connected with youth, are partly designed to avert the dangers of 'marrying out'. . . Our long history of Diaspora existence has taught us how to be Jewish in the face of persecution. But we have not yet learnt how to remain loyal to our Jewish heritage in the open society. Therefore, the greatest danger to Jewish survival outside Israel today is not anti-Semitism but assimilation, epitomised by the threat of intermarriage. . . Intermarriage is a direct threat to Judaism, for without Jews Judaism cannot exist.[4]

Marmur muses on the paradox that the very acceptance Jews craved for through the centuries of exile now tthreatens their existence as a people, and concludes that only a thorough-going rediscovery of what Judaism really stands for will preserve authentic Jewish existence. In a recent book he continues his probing with the question 'What do Jews want to survive *for*?'[5]

Once the initial years of adjustment are completed many Asians will be asking the same question. At present communal solidarity is fuelled by the need to stand together against racial discrimination, and the mosque and the gurdwara can easily become buildings with more of an ethnic than a religious purpose. Rejected by white society, Asians naturally retreat to the centre which affirms them as people of significance. It would not be wise to assume that racial prejudice is being eliminated by statute or common opinion. Attacks on Jewish synagogues, as well as on Asian and Caribbean people are alarmingly frequent, and discrimination in the scramble for employment leaves black people seriously disadvantaged. But it may be that in time such wrongs will come to seem a thing of the past, and black people will find the same kind of acceptance as Jews do today, though it is doubtful that they can ever be as 'invisible' as today's European Jews. Once this happens, Asians will be faced with the same question that now faces Jews; what makes us different? What do we want to be different *for*?

I have introduced these points in a chapter on marriage and the family because the family, with marriage as its linchpin, is the basic unit in society, and the Jewish problem of intermarriage today could be many other people's problem tomorrow.

The character of a marriage creates the character of the next generation, which is why Jews are so worried about their future as a people. Will the character of Muslims, Hindus and Sikhs as religious communities in the West be similarly threatened in years to come?

Already there are a considerable number of marriages which I shall call 'mixed-faith marriages'. (In much of what follows I am drawing on my *Mixed-faith Marriage. A Case for Care*.[6]) In these, people of nominal or real Christian faith have married Muslims (mainly), Sikhs and Hindus, occasionally adopting the faith of their spouse, but more often retaining a kind of allegiance to what they understand of Christianity. As with the Jewish case, where it is generally Jewish men who marry non-Jewish girls, (or so Marmur states in his pamphlet), it is generally Asian men who marry white girls, since as we have seen before the Asian girl is usually prevented by her parents wherever possible from making the kind of relationships which might lead to a marriage which her parents had not arranged. Her brother will have more freedom. In other respects, however, there are contrasts. Jews 'marrying out' are usually thought of as lost to Judaism, especially when the man does so, since Jewish identity is traced through a Jewish mother. If the mother is not Jewish, the children cannot be either, whatever the pedigree of their father. In addition, since much Jewish worship and ritual observance takes place in the home, and in the kitchen in particular, a non-Jewish mother is much less likely to preserve a 'kosher' home, indeed in most Jewish minds would be unable to do so by definition (see chapter 3). In Israel non-Jewish girls marrying Jewish men generally convert to Judaism, on pain otherwise of having their children regarded as illegitimate.

Islam, however, does envisage the possibility of marriage between Muslims and those of non-Muslim faith, and lays down that only the Muslim man should do so, not the Muslim girl, and that the non-Muslim wife should belong to the 'people of the Book', which is usually interpreted as meaning Jews and Christians. Far from being 'lost to Islam' it is presumed that the children of the marriage will be brought up as Muslim and in fact, according to Muslim law, cannot inherit from their father unless they are. (Non-Muslims may not inherit from Muslims, and vice-versa). As we have seen, the bride joins her husband's family in Muslim tradition, and in many ways ceases to belong to her own. The children she bears belong to that family and under Muslim law she has the right of custody only during their infancy, in the event of being widowed or divorced. In addition, non-Muslim girls marrying Muslims in the West are sometimes urged to adopt Islam themselves, for the Muslim in-laws feel that this will strengthen the marriage and ensure the proper Muslim character of the new generation.

At present it is very unclear what the general outcome of these marriages will be. There are cases where a couple have married at a time when neither felt any obligation to their respective religious tradition. Religion simply did not concern them in their daily lives, and therefore the difference between their religious backgrounds seemed to be unimportant to their marriage. Later however, the Muslim husband was influenced by friends from the mosque to take a much more active part in its life. Under the pressure of the prejudice shown against him as an Asian and the dogged certainties of his friends, he began to search for his cultural roots and found them in Islam. But the life of a devout Muslim, like that of an observant Jew, demands an avoidance of pork and alcohol, and a number of other laws relating to food and hygiene which are alien and bothersome to the average Westerner. The wife did not take kindly to this new life-style her husband had adopted, neither did what she knew of Islam through Western newspapers (see chapter 9) fill her with any enthusiam. The result was a new and unwelcome strain on their marriage.

Marriage, where so much is invested, is always a potential source of disillusionment and unimagined disappointments, but marriage across cultural and religious frontiers obviously carries extra risks. But it is not for these reasons that almost every religious community advises against marrying out of one's religious inheritance. We have seen how Jews fear the steady erosion of their community by intermarriage. Among some reform synagogues of the United States this has led to a radically new policy of Jews actually seeking to win the non-Jewish spouses of Jews to Judaism. We have seen this is customary in Israel, but in the Diaspora (Jewish world outside Israel) would-be converts to Judaism have often been repelled at first with the question 'Whatever makes you want to become a Jew?' No move to seek converts has been made previously by Jews since the early centuries of the Christian era, for in the face of the Christian persecution of Jews, that would have added seriously to their troubles.

Muslims accept intermarriage on their own terms. Provided the Islamic character of the family is not put at risk, it is permissible. But only the husband is thought capable of providing that safeguard. A Muslim wife in a non-Muslim home might have to endure licentious talk about the Prophet and other insults to her faith. The prohibition on her marriage to a non-Muslim means that if the husband of a Muslim couple is converted to a faith other than Islam, for example Christianity, the marriage is regarded in Muslim law as automatically dissolved. In some countries this situation has led a few unscrupulous people to procure the formal submission to Islam of a Christian girl, whereupon her previous, valid marriage to a Christian becomes null and void and she is free to marry her Muslim admirer, which of course was the whole point of the exercise.

Hindus, as is well known, normally marry only within caste loyalties, but if these are to be broken at all, Hindu sensibility will not jib at marriage with someone from another faith altogether, for in that understanding all religions are about the same basic thing. In fact, since a non-Indian is clearly outside the structure of caste altogether, it may actually be easier to marry a devout foreigner than someone from a much lower caste. But high-caste Hindu parents would be unhappy at someone whose personal life was morally questionable, a habitual drinker, or someone engaged in an unclean occupation, for example a butcher. Sikhs share many of the same attitudes as Hindus though they formally reject the caste system, and have consistently resisted the pull of Hindu custom on their own way of life. Sikhs, both in the West and in India itself, are a minority community and therefore vulnerable to the erosion of their community through intermarriage, especially of a daughter, with outsiders. Sikhs, in their view, should marry Sikhs, for the *Guru Granth Sahib*, the Sikh scripture, says 'They are not man and wife who have physical contact only. Only they are truly wedded who have one spirit in two bodies.'[7] However, it is possible for those outside the community to become Sikhs, and there is some evidence to suggest that this is preferred by the Sikh community in the West, when a mixed-faith marriage is in prospect.

It remains to consider Christian attitudes. As the largest religious community in Western countries Christians do not normally think of the church itself as vulnerable, as Jews and Sikhs do, to erosion by intermarriage. Moreover Christian women through nearly twenty centuries have shown a re-markable power of influence over their unbelieving husbands. Especially in the early centuries Christian queens were re-sponsible for the conversion of their husbands, and through them of the whole of a nation. Clotilda, who married Clovis, king of the Franks in 493, and Bertha, wife of King Ethelbert of Kent who welcomed the missionary Augustine to England in 597 — such women profoundly affected the whole of European history. So did Monica, mother of the more famous Augustine of North Africa, who prayed her son through to Christian faith in spite of his unbelieving father. But such mixed-faith marriages were often dynastic affairs, or otherwise arranged without the real involvement of the woman con-cerned. Christian men or women of today would be extremely unwise to enter the very different circumstances of marriage in the modern West with the private intention of converting their partners to their own faith. Marriage in Christian under-standing is a complete self-giving to the other, and it is difficult to see how this can exist side-by-side with a consistent pressure for the conversion of the other.

Some would argue that this betrays a misunderstanding of evangelism, and that to place oneself totally at the service of another, as in marriage, does not in any way make it impossible to desire and work and pray for their conversion. It is true that Paul seems to have much the same thought in mind when he counsels Christian partners in marriage to pagans.[8] But he is writing to people converted *after* their marriage, not to people whose marriage was part of their conscious obedience to Jesus Christ from the beginning. For those yet to marry his advice was in line with Jewish practice:

'Do not unite yourselves with unbelievers; they are no fit mates for you.'[9] (However, it is not clear that his principal concern in the passage was marriage – see the varied translations.) In Old Testament times marriage with non-Jews had acquired a sinister reputation through Ahab's marriage with Jezebel, and even Solomon's many foreign alliances were blamed for the idolatry prevalent in his court. After the Jews returned from exile in Babylon Ezra and Nehemiah tackled the problem vigorously, and although the book of Ruth reminded Jews that David himself numbered a Moabitess among his ancestors, the prohibition remained. Christians may have recalled that John the Baptist was executed through the intervention of Herodias, who could not tolerate his criticism of her marriage as improper in Jewish law.

It may seem absurd to drag in the dancing Salome to a discussion of whether Christians should marry those of other faiths today, but the story may serve as a reminder that much more is involved in marriage than the relationship between two people. The continuity of the human race is also involved. Our children present us with questions and issues, as Herod found, that we might choose not to face for ourselves. If children come from two religious communities, where do they belong? I once met a Jamaican who told me his father was Jewish and his mother was Christian. 'What was I?' he said. 'I had to find out. The answer was to become a Muslim.' It was an answer he declared himself very satisfied with, but one wonders how many children of such unions grow up with an indifference to all religion as a result of the difference between their parents.

People often assume that mixed-*faith* marriages and mixed-*race* marriages are on the same footing here, for of course many marriages are both. With the characteristic Western casualness to religious issues they assume that the difference of faith is no more significant than the difference of skin-colour. If you do not ask what race a child from a mixed-*race* marriage is, why should you inquire where a child of mixed-*faith* parentage belongs? He or she is a child, and that is enough. But one of the major themes of this book is the significance of religious choice, of self-understanding within a religious framework. You do not choose what colour your skin is. Nothing you can do will change it. That is why racial discrimination is such blatant evil, for it attempts to destroy the unity of the human race. It is an attack on common humanity. But faith can be chosen, and if it is to be authentic faith *must* be chosen. That choice must be respected, and society must frame its laws to take as much account as possible of minority faiths so that people are enabled to live by their conviction in freedom. But the microcosmic society which is marriage and the family cannot, it seems to me, have pluralism at its heart. It must be clear about the fundamentals, in Christian terms who is Lord. If there is no agreement about what is fundamental I do not see how a marriage can fulfil its potential, or be other than an unequal partnership of conflicting senses of identity. In practice many mixed-faith marriages end in the virtual capitulation of one religious identity to the other.

What is said above should not be read as meaning that Christians have nothing to learn about marriage from others. Here, as elsewhere, the kaleidoscope of cultures reminds us of much that we had forgotten, or never properly known. Other cultures have in some ways stayed closer to a biblical perspective. Germaine Greer, author and pioneer feminist, compares India with the West, and is appalled by the way families in the West treat their children. 'Maybe it's guilt. But deep down, it is really because we don't like children.' And because we don't really like children, she says, we no longer have them.[10] And with children out of the way, there is no urgent need to preserve marriage either. So a generation which does not believe in itself or anything else does not even bother to ensure its own continuity. But so also, in the mercy of God, the East provokes the West to rediscover its roots, and the source of all creativity.

Chapter Six

Health and Handicap

A British couple living abroad were called back to their house one day by a distraught child-minder. Their five-year-old son, the only child, had been playing with a faulty light fitting and electrocuted himself. As I and other anxious friends called to try to share their sorrow, someone asked their doctor whether the grief-stricken parents should be given some tranquillizing pills. 'No,' he said. 'They have to begin to live with the fact of his death sooner or later.'

It seemed at first a harsh response, for they faced a harrowing journey back to Britain with the body and the prospect of a total change in their lives. But we cannot be anaesthetized from reality to live in a world of troubled dreams. Sometimes it seems as though the West regards pain as the greatest of evils and its elimination as the one aim of life. Yet there is much pain and distress, both in the mind and the body, which can only be lived with and dealt with day by day. No magic pills exist to remove it. Every person and every society has to cope with circumstances and problems which are not open to instant solutions of any sort, and the question then becomes how to find powers and resources for creative endurance. Life in the West, with the rapidity of its communications and the amazing development of its technology, seems to promise cures for every ill. But neither chemical nor mechanical answers can deal with the deep inner pain of sudden bereavement. The limitations imposed by mental or physical handicap bring a sense of being useless and devalued which no gadgetry can overcome. Many sorrows, pains and weaknesses have to be lived with, and endurance based on hope is the only real means of coping with them. Pills and crutches of various kinds may help, but nothing can replace the ability to sustain, sometimes over many years, an inner vitality which refuses to be trapped in hopelessness and despair.

Sometimes people speak of the resignation and fatalism of the East, and by contrast of the analytical, problem-solving skills of Western people. But to many caught up in situations of severe disability or chronic illness, of multiple disadvantage or sudden, crippling catastrophe, neither the resigned acceptance of the one nor the analysis of the other will help. Acceptance may blind one to opportunities of altering the situation. Analysis of the evil may equally make its solution seem totally unattainable. It is possible to know too much about one's problems, so that analysis brings paralysis. Both in the life of the individual and in the life of society it is endurance and hope which produce change. These things concern the mysterious thing we call the 'morale' of a person or a group, their vitality or in older language, their 'spirit'. In the broadest sense the struggle with illness or handicap or tragedy is a spiritual one. That being so, it would be surprising if the religious traditions of the world did not have much to say about it.

People who know their circumstances as on the edge of what is tolerable need a community, a reason and a vision. They need first of all a sense of not being alone, of not being cut off from normal human society, that there are others who care and will help. Often the desolation of bereavement is accentuated by the sense of being odd man out. After my father's death my mother told me that she felt people were avoiding her, crossing the road not to meet her and saying to each other 'There's Mrs Lamb – she's just lost her husband.' I think it is unlikely that they were, but C. S. Lewis writes of something similar in his *A Grief Observed*, first published under another name after his wife's death:

> I'm aware of being an embarrassment to everyone I meet. . . R. has been avoiding me for a week. . . To some I'm worse than an embarrassment. I am a death's head. Wherever I meet a happily married pair I can feel them both thinking 'One or other of us must some day be as he is now'.[1]

The British Broadcasting Corporation runs a radio programme for the handicapped called *Does He Take Sugar?* which neatly expresses the same sense that the sufferer is somehow cut off from ordinary society, perhaps best approached through a third person. Of course the inquiry about sugar may simply be a wrong assessment of a person's disability, the kind of thoughtlessness shown when deaf people are regarded as stupid or slow-witted. But C. S. Lewis, with his 'death's head' remark, points us to something deeper. Sometimes the person to whom misfortune happens is so associated with that ill that it is feared he will bring it upon others. A classic example is the leper. So the sufferer experiences the double misfortune of the original ill plus the segregation it earns him from the rest of 'normal' society. Clinical separation from other people may be necessary in the case of infectious disease, but what I am speaking about goes much further. The prophet Isaiah describes a mysterious figure who was 'tormented and humbled by suffering', but says that far from being moved by his suffering 'we despised him, we held him of no account, a thing from which men turn away their eyes'.[2]

In some societies mentally handicapped children are hidden away from the outside world by families who regard them as a source of shame to the healthy members, and a threat to their marriage prospects. As well as being unfortunate themselves they are a cause of misfortune to others. Sometimes this stigma of misfortune can attach itself to those whose only problem is to be the bearers of bad news. In Shakespeare's *Antony and Cleopatra* the queen is informed of the marriage of her lover. 'Hence, horrible villain!' she says to the messenger and physically attacks him. According to the stage directions she 'hales him up and down'. She declares,

Though it be honest,
it is never good to bring bad news.
Give to a gracious message
An host of tongues; but let ill tidings tell
Themselves when they be felt. . .

It would be better, she implies, for the honest man to keep a proper distance between misfortune, even that of other people, and himself. In her anguish she lashes out at this particular honest man;

Is he married?
I cannot hate thee worser than I do
If thou again say 'Yes'.[3]

Cleopatra's messenger needed the protection of a community from his queen. Those who live by a religious tradition have often provided that companionship in the face of misfortune. I vividly remember student days in Pakistan when our whole class would go to pay our respects to the family of one of our number whose father had died. We sat with other mourners who were coming and going in the house, exchanging very few words but simply reassuring the bereaved family of our care and our prayers by the mere fact that we had bothered to go and spend twenty minutes with them. Hardly anything was said, but our very presence was eloquent of concern. It is difficult to imagine students in a Western university acting in such a body, or see them joining in brief prayers on return to the lecture room. But death, for these Pakistanis, was a common encounter and they knew instinctively that its bewildering isolation was best combatted by a determined solidarity.

When, later on, our eldest daughter died in Pakistan at the age of eight we were grateful for the friends and acquaintances who came to sit quietly with us, to laugh or cry as our mood suggested. The poorest of them, no strangers to death in the family, sat by preference on the floor and offered us their love in silence as we had done to our fellow-student. We learnt that while friends would forgive your absence from a wedding every effort had to be made to attend a funeral, even though it generally took place within twenty-four hours of death. At least you should visit the family at the earliest opportunity. We found in contrast that some of our Western friends found it difficult even to mention the subject of our daughter's death. We didn't, of course, expect or want a debate about it, merely an acknowledgement of the scale and significance of what had happened. Many Westerners today will not trust themselves so much as to mention death in any serious conversation.

The solidarity expressed in grief in Pakistan is expressed in sickness also. A sick person expects to be visited, and may well play to the gallery in displaying his symptoms. This we found less welcome when we were ill, for the British instinct prefers to be left alone, to be ill in peace. My wife, in the throes of typhoid, heaved herself up on her pillows and tried to smile at visitors she didn't really want to see at all. A Pakistani patient would probably have lain back and groaned without restraint, but then their visitors would have relished the drama, whereas our Britishness had taught us only embarrassment in the face of noisy suffering. The famous 'stiff upper lip' let us down, for the sense of being unwelcome must have communicated itself to those who had taken the trouble to come to see us.

Western patterns of health care tend to isolate the patient in antiseptic loneliness. Of course many others are around, and in fact uncomfortably close, but they are strangers who only exceptionally convey the warmth of family care. To an Asian woman arriving in the West from the Indian sub-continent, perhaps having a baby within the first year, the hospital surroundings are public, frightening and inexplicable. In many places there are few interpreters, and the staff have been given little opportunity to learn about the very different customs of Asian people in health and sickness. An Urdu-speaking Christian woman tells of one experience:

A seventeen year old bride of less than a year arrived to join her husband in this country. She was already pregnant. Two days later she was admitted into hospital and delivered a full-term baby. Because of the danger of infection before arrival, she was quite properly put in a single room and barrier-nursed, and the other patients were told not to go near her. Sister was very worried about her. The girl neither spoke nor understood English, she had never met her in-laws till she came to this country, she had never been alone in a room in her life, and she was terrified, cowering in bed and shrinking away when anyone approached. The staff wondered if they should arrange for her to be seen by a psychiatrist. When I greeted her in Urdu, she burst into tears, and I asked 'What is your trouble?' She couldn't understand the reason for her isolation and thought she must be very wicked when other Pakistanis were forbidden to visit her. I explained the reasons and she was happier about it, but then I went on to talk of God, using the lovely Urdu expression 'Hazir-o-Nazir' – Present and Seeing, and that even when she was alone in a room in the dark, God was still present and seeing, still awake and watching. And so she was comforted.

Luke records that Jesus 'gave the twelve apostles power and authority to overcome all the devils and to cure diseases, and sent them to proclaim the Kingdom of God and to heal'.[4] Here was a Christian woman doing precisely that, for what greater dis-ease can there be than the prospect of pain and isolation culminating in the fear, however irrational it might seem, that you are identified with evil. Cleopatra's messenger did not enjoy that situation, and he was not in hospital.

The Pakistani girl in the incident recounted above felt happier as soon as she knew the reason for her isolation from other patients, though it must still have seemed very strange to her. We must have some framework of interpretation into which we can fit the various things that happen to us. When what happens is painful or even tragic, the question 'Why' insists on some sort of answer. Hindus will often answer in terms of *karma*, the universal moral law by which evil deeds have their sure result in later accident, failure or misfortune. Roger Hooker records a Hindu friend as saying,

> *Karma* explains everything. If I cut my finger or a friend addresses me angrily, that means I have paid off the debt incurred by some past offence. . . Why should I want forgiveness? Is it not better to suffer the punishment for what I have done? In that way I can wipe off the entail of the past and begin my next life with a clean slate.[5]

Others may see some grave illness as the result of the intervention of a god. Smallpox has often been attributed to the Hindu goddess Shītala Devi. The gods do not have to account for their actions, and are as capricious in the minds of their twentieth-century devotees as they are in the myths of ancient Greece and Rome. They are human beings writ large, and if they 'take against' you it is wisest to submit and plead for their favour to return, or for another more powerful god to intervene. Jews and Muslims, as well as Christians, may scoff at such superstition in the modern world, but it does offer a framework of interpretation, something for bewildered people to hang on to, and hence its persistence. Peter Speck, an experienced hospital chaplain, writes that observation has shown that those with a strong religious faith, and those with deeply-held humanist convictions alike face death and serious loss with calmness and a sense of dignity.

> Those who are unsure, lukewarm and hazy in their religious beliefs and who only attend a place of worship for a 'hatch, match and dispatch' ministry are the ones who exhibit most anxiety in relation to dying.[6]

This is only to observe what apparently happens, not to justify any explanation as better than none. The fact is that people are frequently taken aback by sudden loss and can find little in their mental and spiritual equipment which has prepared them for it. But we shall all die, and many of us will experience sudden changes in our circumstances which bring much suffering. We need to think through the meaning of suffering as far as we can, if possible *before* it hits us. Not that we should turn 'suffering' into a concept, an abstract term to be tossed from mouth to mouth and mind to mind. Nowhere do we have to tread more carefully than in speaking about suffering in the presence of those who know its greater depths. Nevertheless we all know some degree of loss and pain. Even if we have not known the death of a close family member there are many occasions when we move from one home or school or job to another, and in each case there is a loss and a bereavement and a necessary stage of readjustment.

Dying is part of living in that we have continually to forego, voluntarily or involuntarily, one set of possibilities in order to pursue another. When that process is under our own control, or seems to be, we probably fail to notice the element of loss and dying that is involved. When someone changes their home or their job for a better one every thought is about the excitement and possibilities of the new. But when choice is forced upon us, when radical changes come through bereavement, illness or unemployment, the new situation seems so cramped and distressing that it is difficult to see anything good about it. In the case of bereavement it often seems disloyal to the dead person, and in the case of incapacitating illness it seems unfeeling or absurd to imagine that there can be any positive element in the situation.

Yet the triumph of certain remarkable people over severe disablement and sickness should make us think again. Dame Cicely Saunders tells us of a patient who was

one of my greatest friends. . . a girl who was only forty years old when she died. For the first years I remember she gradually became paralyzed and blind and for the last three years was totally without sight and almost without any movement at all. Many of us came to be her friends, but it was another patient who best summed up what one saw in her as she lived on in the midst of this slow dying of her body. As she came away from her bedside one afternoon this patient said to us, 'The incredible thing is, you don't even feel sorry for her: she is *so* alive.' Her dying had become the very means of her growth, for we learnt from her husband that her intense aliveness, gaiety and interest in other people had developed during her illness. Always we remember her laughter, made more vivid by the occasional tears that showed us how much this cost her. The less her body could do the more her spirit shone, in love and amusement and a clear-sighted wisdom concerning life and those she met.[7]

It is obvious that many factors may combine to prevent such a triumph of spirit over circumstances. The dying patient is sometimes regarded as a medical failure, and doctors and nurses are reluctant to visit them, as Mary Baines records.[8] The Cleopatra syndrome! The patient him- or herself may never have received enough care and love in their past life to enable them to respond creatively to such a crisis. Their last days may be absorbed by anxiety about those who will be left behind. But the potential is there in human beings. How is it to be realized?

Cicely Saunders speaks out of her pioneer experience of the hospice movement of the 'truth of the mind in skill and understanding with truth of the heart in vulnerable friendship.'[9] At first sight 'vulnerable friendship' is not a promising way to deal with loss and pain and death. How does it help for someone else to be caught up in my problems? Why should I drag others down with me? So the sufferer may feel. From the side of the 'healthy' helper, there is often a need to avoid the one in trouble. 'I'm sorry but there is nothing I can do. I can't get involved.' As we saw above even professional medical personnel, whose job is caring for the sick, may come to view some patients as reminders of their own failure and inadequacy as healers, and so avoid personal contact with them. Yet the friendships made by Cicely Saunders and others, which have grown into the hospice movement, and the solidarity in suffering which we saw among Pakistanis at the beginning of this chapter, do make all the difference to the sufferer. What is the vision of such friendship and such solidarity? What is the engine which moves a distant pity into active compassion?

I feel it can only be a conviction that this is somehow the way that the world is meant to operate – this is how it was made to run. Such a vision may be barely articulate, or it may be expressed in the traditional language of the world's religions. Muslims pray to Allah as 'the compassionate, the merciful'; Jews celebrate the *hesed* (steadfast love) of the Master of the Universe; Buddhists speak of the compassion which marks the way of enlightenment; the motto of the All-India Jaina Association is 'Love Conquers All.' But what kind of love is this? What is the nature of a love which is adequate for the sort of world we live in? The Chinese Christian theologian Choan-Seng Song tells us that in Chinese

> one is required to say the two words *love* and *pain* almost in the same breath. I am referring to the expression pain-love (*thun-ai*). . . A mother feels pain-love for her child. Husband and wife feel pain-love for each other. Inherent in such a pain-love is self-sacrifice. Through the intensely human experience of pain-love we can surmise what God's love for the world may be like. . . The cross is God's excruciating pain-love. It is rooted in the love of the God who bears pain for the world.[10]

Cicely Saunder's 'vulnerable friendship' could then be another name for the love of God, as this Chinese Christian sees it. Together with the medical skill of appropriate treatment and nursing ('the truth of the mind') this vision of the pain-love of God is a 'truth of the heart' which energizes compassion and creative endurance.

But the vision needs to go further. Care in itself, however caring, will ease but cannot finally reconcile the sufferer to his loss, unless there can be some hope that the loss will ultimately be restored, or else utterly transcended. Here the Christian experience of the resurrection is decisive. When our daughter died someone said to us 'God knows how you feel. It happened to him.' But if that were all, we should be no better off. God, being God, must be able to resolve the agonizing discord into harmony. Or else the world is like Edvard Munch's picture *The Cry*, in which a woman on a bridge opens her mouth in endless terror.

To say that the world's discord, the world's scream, *must* be resolved and healed, is not in strict logic to say that it will or can be. Logically the possibility must be faced, if it ever can be, that the world is a torture-chamber with no exit. God, if he exists, is a cosmic sadist. C. S. Lewis, in the depths of his anguish, faced that thought as his prayers for his wife were apparently ignored. But he rejected it because a being like that

> couldn't invent or create or govern anything. He would set traps and try to bait them. But he'd never have thought of baits like love, or laughter, or daffodils, or a frosty sunset. *He* make a universe? He couldn't make a joke, or a bow, or an apology, or a friend.[11]

The yearnings of religious people for millenia have not been futile, nor will the human story in all its beauty and its tragedy end in mocking laughter. Christians are convinced that through the resurrection of Jesus Christ God has shown the full effect of his pain-love for all his creatures. Now, in that knowledge, everyone can lift up their heads in hope. In the Revelation of John the whole purpose of God's creation is seen to be a community of love, and at the heart of the throne of God, in the very midst of it all, is a lamb 'with the marks of slaughter upon him'.[12] There can be no doubt that this is Jesus, who earlier says to John, 'Do not be afraid. I am the first and the last, and I am the living one; for I was dead and now I am alive for evermore, and I hold the keys of Death and Death's domain.'[13] At the end of the book a loud voice proclaims from the throne:

> Now at last God has his dwelling among men! He will dwell among them and they shall be his people, and God himself will be with them. He will wipe every tear from their eyes; there shall be an end to death, and to mourning and crying and pain; for the old order has passed away![14]

Meanwhile, although, as Christians believe, the old order is doomed, it has not yet passed away, and we are called to live in faith. What will this mean in practice as far as health and handicap are concerned? It must mean a readiness to go *through* suffering rather than round it, to face the full reality of loss and deprivation instead of trying somehow to hide from it. For Jesus has proved that there is nothing to fear in God's final purposes. On our way to the new order we pick up every kind of clue and try to learn from every source what a fully healed and health-full human life must be like. Western society, in spite of its amazing advances in medicine, is hardly a model of wholeness. Many from Asian religious traditions would find fault with the mechanical view of the human body implied in many of its health practices. A Western patient goes to his or her doctor with specific complaints, presenting definite symptoms even when these prove minor in comparison with the real trouble. An Asian patient, to the frustration of his Western doctor, may simply say 'I am not doing my work. I have pain everywhere.' The Asian patient expects his doctor not only to diagnose his illness but also to divine his symptoms, and then of course to treat him. He is unimpressed by further investigations or lengthy questioning.

Clearly such attitudes partly derive from a traditional society in which people understand little in any scientific sense of the working of their own bodies, and consequently place excessive trust in the local practitioners of herbal and other systems of medicine. But it is also possible that they have preserved a greater grasp of their own wholeness as body/spirit people. They do not divide up their bodies and say that there is pain here but not here. The whole body is affected by pain in one part, just as the whole community mourns when one member is bereaved. It is the same kind of mental world as that described by John V. Taylor in his account of a night spent working with African fishermen on Lake Victoria. They were pulling nets in from the water:

> One man, passing me on his way down to the water rubbed a hand over his sore shoulders. 'We have the same pain', I murmured to him. 'And one power', he grunted, clutching the rope again behind me. For the second time I felt the edges of separateness evaporating.[15]

The same sense of the wholeness of the human body is seen in the almost universal distaste of Asian people for post-mortems, to which relatives will agree only if it is a legal necessity. A frequent request is that all organs removed from the body should be replaced before burial or cremation. Many, especially Muslims, would not believe it right to authorize the removal of eyes or kidneys from a dead relation even to benefit a living patient, much less hypothetical advances in medical research. The sense of life's wholeness under God also produces a profound antipathy to abortion. The human body, in this view, is not a piece of property entirely at the disposal of its owner. Life is generally thought to begin at conception and the mother who protects that life is not at liberty to end it. Normal family planning, however, is gaining ground steadily, despite conservative opposition, especially amoung Muslims. The International Planned Parenthood Federation has produced a pamphlet called *Islam and Family Planning* which quotes from distinguished Muslim jurists in its favour, but there are many Muslims who still believe it to be forbidden. Details of these and many other religious attitudes to health care can be found in the invaluable booklet *Religions and Cultures*.[16]

When the 'edges of separateness' begin to evaporate the Westerner is often alarmed, just as he is puzzled by those for whom they do not exist. The ideas of individual separateness and independence have had a long run in Western societies, and one result has been a large measure of personal freedom. But Christians who take the Bible seriously are constantly reminded that its viewpoint is a corporate one, and its vision of the fulfilment of all God's purposes is a heavenly city. 'God said, "It is not good for the man to be alone".'[17] God chose a people, and Jesus selected twelve men to represent the restoration of that people. Paul spoke of the church as Christ's body, and declared that 'if one organ suffers, they all suffer together'.[18] Is God not calling us to rethink many of our attitudes and the habits and organizations, medical and other, that they have brought about?

Chapter Seven

Morality and Law

Priest: Do you renounce evil?
Answer: I renounce evil.
The Alternative Service Book, 1980, Service of Baptism

Few religious people would have any difficulty in answering
this particular question in the new Church of England baptism service. Like the man who preached about sin, we can be
sure that they are against it. The real problem is how to deal
with evil or sin when it arises – how the person or people can
be convinced of their guilt and the damage done by the offence
as far as possible put right. It is often said that we live in a
very immoral age, or that the West at least is 'permissive'.
However there is no absence of moral fervour from public life.
People in democratic countries protest loudly about any
number of things – the iniquity of nuclear weapons, the
poverty of millions, the inequality of wages, racial discrimination, the injustice done to Palestinians, the injustice done to
Jews, the injustice done to innumerable other national groups,
the promiscuity of the young, the corruption of the old, the
right to abortion, the slaughter of the unborn, cruelty to
animals, cruelty to political opponents – the list is endless.
There is hardly an issue seriously debated in public life which
is not at heart a moral one. Morality, injustice and oppression
are what propel a remarkable number of people into action.
'It's wrong!' they say.

What has certainly happened in many Western countries is
that the focus and character of moral judgements has
changed. 'Sin' is a word which has lost much of its older
richness of meaning and is often popularly used as equivalent
to sexual licence. 'Morality' also chiefly implies the area of
personal and especially sexual ethics. If you want to create a
stir by attacking a public figure you call him 'corrupt', or
'bent' rather than 'immoral', since corruption is recognized as
an offence with broader implications than the private character associated with 'morality'. The focus of moral perception

has changed, and many Western people are confused by the change, especially the elderly. The explanation may be that the change simply reflects a greater prominence given to social rather than personal morality – something traditionally associated with 'working-class solidarity'.

Asian people who have come to live in the West have a strong sense of personal morality inculcated by their religious values, but they are not always perceived as moral people by the Westerners among whom they settle. The white headmistress of a Midlands primary school with a high proportion of Asian children told me in all seriousness: 'The trouble is that these children have no sense of right and wrong.' A few careful conversations with some of her parents should have put her right, but she had not foreseen that these children might have a *different* sense of right and wrong. Being children, they were unable to perceive the difference themselves and articulate it. Even a broader experience of British society might have convinced her that several different understandings of morality may co-exist in one country, without taking racial or ethnic differences into account. Among working-class people it has long been thought immoral to help employers break a strike by continuing to work. 'Scab' or 'blackleg' is more than a term of abuse. It carries a moral connotation as well. Similarly the person who works conspicuously harder than his fellows may be accused of creating difficulties for the whole work-force by raising the expectations of management.

This kind of morality is easily identified as a morality determined by theories, or the experience, of class warfare. From another part of the political spectrum come equally identifiable sentiments. A Conservative member of parliament attacked the Church of England in parliament in July, 1981, declaring that it was the loss of the old values of loyalty, love of one's parents and country and discipline which had led to problems in industry and elsewhere and to the recent bloody riots. 'Unless', he said, 'the bishops can grasp these points, can abandon their old ways and give a lead to the return of decency and morality, I see little help for England.'[1]

There is a clear assumption here than not only are certain personal moral issues at the heart of the national welfare, but that the leaders of institutional Christianity have a particular responsibility to engage with them on behalf of the nation as a whole. When the Church of England began, like other churches, to concentrate less on private and personal moral issues and took a more corporate view of morality its leaders were called 'trendy lefties', people who had politicized religion. Here is a thorny subject, on which one might argue that religion, if it is not to be an entirely private and therefore extremely limited obligation, is inevitably politicized and always has been. I hope to show that once we consider other religions as well as Christianity, this becomes very obvious. On the Christian faith itself and its political significance John Habgood has written with characteristic lucidity:

A Gospel which belongs to the world of public discourse, which it must if it is to be credible, cannot fail to have relevance to public life as well as to private life. To this extent a high degree of social awareness in Christianity is unavoidable. But how ought it to be expressed in Britain today? . . . The involvement, it is constantly said, should be moral rather than political. (But) the distinction is easier to draw in theory than in practice.[2]

Here we may leave for the moment the question of the church's political involvement to note simply that people's ideas about morality are profoundly affected by their social and political standpoint.

In the West, however, there are certain common assumptions made by most, if not all those who use the words 'right' and 'wrong'. However developed our 'social awareness' we think of morality as properly distinguished from the public law of the land. It is at least to that extent a 'private' matter. There are actions which are widely recognized by a variety of moral codes as immoral but are not actually a legal offence. Adultery is immoral but it has never been a crime in British law, nor is there any lobby which would want to make it so. People generally recognize that there is a whole area of morally dubious behaviour which is not subject to legal restriction. Sometimes this is due to the impossibility of enforcing laws against, for example, shady financial transactions, rather than an agreement that this or that is an area of behaviour which should not be controlled by law. However, there is continual rethinking going on of what behaviour should be subject to legal penalties and what should not. Proposals have been made to establish guidelines for controlling the activity of religious 'cults'. These concern guarantees of access to members of the group by family and friends, the open identification of religious movements during recruitment, and the right of recruits to seek independent advice and medical help. These have all been matters of recent concern for those involved with such groups. The proposals have understandably been opposed because they could threaten hardly won religious freedoms for everyone. But it is worth noting that their supporters make it clear that the right to religious *belief*, however bizarre, is not in question. 'If people want to say God is an orange and lives in a dustbin, that's up to them.'[3] It could be argued that earlier in British history the concerns of the law would have been expressed in exactly the opposite way. The law prohibiting blasphemy (still on the statute book) would have been invoked as sufficient reason for banning such groups altogether, without the niceties of compelling them to grant freedom of access to the relatives of members. The compulsory wearing of car seat-belts, legislation to control and restrict the advertizing of cigarettes, the laws against the incitement of racial hatred, the laws designed to promote equality of opportunity between the sexes – all these are recent British examples of behaviour which was 'right' or at least permitted, and is now 'wrong'. On the other side, especially in sexual morality, actions such as private homosexual behaviour between consenting adults, and abortion, which were 'wrong' are not now subject to legal penalty.

There is always, of course, a mismatch between statute law and the prevailing concepts of morality. But if the gulf is too wide, either the law is openly flouted – as with the use of cannabis in some countries – or the public credibility of a moral code suffers and its directives become regarded as merely private and irrational scruples. In Britain this seems to be happening very rapidly to the old prohibition against sexual intercourse before marriage, and even outside marriage. Many Asian newcomers to Britain, as is well known, feel that the moral standards of the West, especially in sexual matters, are deplorably low. What is less well known is that Muslims in particular, and some from other religious tradi-

tions, regard law and morality as derived from the same
source, the will of God. In Pakistan I had many times to try to
explain the new British legal position (as it was then) regard-
ing homosexuality, but the distinction between crime and sin
was strange to those I spoke to. A crime, I said, was generally
a sin, except under a very corrupt government, but not every
sin was, or should be a crime. As the Wolfenden Report said:

Unless a deliberate attempt is to be made by society. . . to
equate the sphere of crime with that of sin, there must
remain a realm of private morality and immorality, which
is, in brief and crude terms, not the law's business.[4]

But I found myself in difficulties with both Muslims and
Pakistani Christians, for, they said, did not both the Bible and
the Qur'an prohibit homosexual activity? Did not both the
Bible and the Qur'an prescribe punishments for sexual mis-
demeanours and sexual perversity? Yes, I said, but. . . They
listened patiently as I tried to describe the idea of a secular
law which was informed by religious understanding but also
open to constant human amendment, but I think I failed to
convince either Muslim or Christian.

I think they assumed that human beings do not make law,
God does. They would have agreed, of course, that human
beings are entrusted with the task of translating God's law
into statute law, but since they lacked any experience as
administrators they did not see much difficulty in that. It
might have helped if I had pointed out to them the difference
between two types of law in the Old Testament, one broadly
corresponding to moral precept and the other framed as a
legal statute. In the book of Exodus, for example, we are told:

When men quarrel and one hits another with a stone or
with a spade, and the man is not killed but takes to his bed;
if he recovers so as to walk about outside with a stick, then
the one who struck him has no liability, except that he shall
pay for loss of time and shall see that he is cured.[5]

This is in the form of a legal enactment, and is technically
known as *casuistic* law. It covers specific conditions, and lays
down what shall happen if the law is broken. But the Old
Testament also contains a great deal of *apodictic* law, notably
in the Ten Commandments. 'Honour your father and your
mother' says the law,[6] but does not tell us how that is to be

done, or what will happen if we fail to do it. The next verse says 'You shall not kill.' Never? Are animals intended to be covered by this law, or enemy soldiers, or murderers themselves? The Israelites clearly did not think so, and other Old Testament laws actually prescribe killing as punishment. Hence the alternative translation of the verse as 'You shall do no murder', which is really an interpretation (as translation often has to be).

Jews have spent tremendous efforts over the centuries in thinking out the practical application of the Torah (the Jewish law). The Jewish religious genius, it has been said, is rooted in concrete situations on earth and therefore takes a legal form, rather than a theological or mystical one. Rabbi Lionel Blue illustrates the point with a story about Elijah ben Solomon Zalman, the famous Lithuanian rabbi of the eighteenth century:

> The learned rabbi was giving a tutorial. Two of his pupils looked out of the window at a bird soaring in the sky. He asked one of them, 'What were you thinking, as you watched the bird?' 'I was thinking of the soul ascending to heaven,' the boy replied. Elijah thought, and asked him to leave his class. He smelt the mysticism of Jewish Poland. He turned to the other boy, and asked him the same question. The boy considered. 'If that bird dropped dead, and fell between two fences,' he said, 'who would own the body?' His teacher replied 'God be praised, for someone knows what religion is about!'[7]

The Muslim religious bent is in this respect very similar to the Jewish, with the added stimulus of the need to review and adjust the customary law of the varied cultures of Muslim lands. Jews, until the modern state of Israel, have had to live as minorities under some alien code of law during the last 2,000 years. This may account for a greater trend towards codification in Muslim law. Many Muslim jurists divide actions into five classes, ranging from what is obligatory, to what is merely recommended, through what is indifferent to what is reprehensible and finally what is prohibited outright. In the middle three categories there is scope for debate, but in the ritual law which is *pre*scribed, and in the category of *pro*scribed actions there is no room for any other judgement.

The Qur'an details five offences which carry fixed penalties, the so-called *hadd* offences. They are: unlawful sexual intercourse, the false accusation of sexual intercourse, the drinking of wine, theft and highway robbery. These, because God has specifically spoken about them in his Word, are thought to be offences against his rights, and therefore no pardon is possible once a case involving one of these issues has been brought before a Muslim judge. If the offender is proved guilty to the satisfaction of the court, nothing but the fixed penalty can be carried out. You will notice the curious fact that offences against property or sexual integrity are regarded as offences against God's rights, whereas violence against the person is not. This is probably because in Muhammad's day murder was avenged by the victim's family, who could accept a sum of money in compensation.[8] Muslims would never say, of course, that God is unconcerned about murder, for the whole of the Shari'a (the law of Islam) is based on divine revelation.

Nevertheless the effect of the specifically Qur'anic injunctions listed above is to throw into prominence the particular offences covered, and to focus Muslim and non-Muslim attention upon them. Western newspapers have frequently made headlines of the grisly tariff of penalties for these offences, stoning for adultery, eighty lashes for the false accusation of adultery and drinking wine, while theft and highway robbery incur the penalty of amputation, either of hand or foot, or even both.[9] What is less often observed is that the conditions for proving adultery are extremely rigorous, nothing less than four adult legally competent male witnesses to the act itself! This is in keeping with the tradition which records the prophet Muhammad as severely restricting the application of all the penalties except for that for false accusation of adultery. This was logical since a case of adultery which was found unproven and therefore dismissed automatically involved the accuser in the penalty of false accusation. Students of the Old Testament will see parallels to the laws detailed in the book of Deuteronomy about malicious witness.[10] Western law, with its Roman origins, knows no such provision, except in the procedures used against policemen accused of 'framing' criminal suspects. Earlier I said that the Midlands headmistress had not perceived that her Asian children might have a different sense of right and wrong from her own. Here is a Semitic example in which the gravity of the law and the seriousness of breaking its provisions is matched by the equal gravity of the process of accusation which must not be lightly or maliciously undertaken. This is underlined, in the same Jewish and Muslim traditions, by the requirement that the punishment of stoning must be begun by the accusers themselves. They are not allowed to shelter behind some 'automatic' machinery of the law, grinding on once they have initiated it. In that sense the law is not impersonal at all, but deeply personal, concerned with the restoration of human relationships.

Nevertheless, however humanely applied and infrequently executed, laws which stipulate lashes, amputation and stoning to death strike a chill note in Western minds. We are not cheered by the reassurance that the strictest medical safe-guards are observed in cases of flogging, or even that the penalty of amputation for theft is so hedged around by conditions about witnesses to the act of taking, the value of the property stolen and the circumstances of the thief (he must not have been in want of food) that it is hardly ever carried out.

Christians are specifically commanded to forgive those who wrong them in the prayer taught by Jesus himself. 'Forgive us our sins as we forgive those who sin against us.' In Matthew's Gospel he records Jesus as underlining the point after he has taught his disciples the prayer: 'For if you forgive others the wrongs they have done, your heavenly Father will also forgive you; but if you do not forgive others, then the wrongs you have done will not be forgiven by your Father.'[11] Matthew records too the parable of the unforgiving debtor,[12] and Luke Jesus' words at the time he was nailed to the cross: 'Father, forgive them; they do not know what they are doing.'[13] Stephen, the first Christian martyr, followed Jesus' example,[14] and Peter commended it to all Christians.[15]

It would be absurd to claim, or even imply that Christians have consistently lived up to this command. Moreover there are serious problems in applying the Christian ethic to public life, as Muslims have often noted. All through history people have found it acceptable, even necessary, to take measures 'for the public good' which they would never dream of adopting in their own private lives. 'For all the centuries of experience, men have not yet learned how to live together without compounding their vices and covering each other "with mud and with blood"' wrote Reinhold Niebuhr in the opening lines of his *Moral Man and Immoral Society*.[16]

Nevertheless the New Testament command to forgive is still there, however much Christians themselves have set it aside, and however difficult it may seem to be to combine it with political wisdom. (Readers with a keen sense of history may recall contrasting attitudes to political 'forgiveness' in the behaviour of two conquerors of Jerusalem: the Crusaders of 1099 who massacred its Jewish and Muslim inhabitants, and the Muslim Saladin in 1187, who displayed a notable magnanimity to the Christian defenders of the city who had resisted him.) If forgiveness is a possibility, in however ideal a world, and actually more, a moral constraint, then the way we cope with wrongdoing will have a different 'feel' about it. But if, being in some position of authority, we may *not* forgive because that would be a mark of weakness or even an infringement of God's rights, then we may not count on anything less than the strictest account from whoever is in the position of judge. Of course parents, teachers, employers, policemen and judges can always be bribed in various ways, or cajoled or pleaded with. But to hope for forgiveness by open confession is likely to be a risky business, since there will be no kind of guarantee that forgiveness will follow the admission of guilt. A friend of mine found some money missing from his home, and questioned a teenage boy who might have known something about it. As he spelt out the circumstantial evidence which pointed to the lad's guilt, he was astonished to find the boy, after first denying all knowledge of the theft, pleading with him to forget about it. 'But you're saying you didn't take the money?' he said, 'No; came the reply; I didn't. Please overlook it this time.' Illogical as it seemed the boy was determined to separate himself from the crime although he could not deny his guilt convincingly.

Of course this is no new thing. Ancient Egyptian texts of prayers to Isis contain detailed repudiations of sin, but no acknowledgement of having actually sinned.[17] This is probably connected with a sense of the uselessness of dwelling on past error, and even a fear that to do so will lead to its repetition. The most one can hope for is that the powerful person or god offended will overlook the offence and treat it as if it had not happened. Raimundo Panikkar, the Catholic scholar of Hinduism, points out that the idea of repentance presupposes a certain understanding of time. It assumes that it is possible to 'turn back', to 'recover', to 'start again', to return to the original starting-point, the lost paradise. It is a radical break with the past, made by taking the past seriously, with all its faults.

> This conception of repentance is hardly possible, or rather understandable, given the notion of time which has prevailed and still prevails in the Indian subcontinent. According to that notion, what has happened has happened and no power on earth or in heaven can undo what has been done. The past cannot be concealed. What Man can do, however, is to handle the future so as to modify it and get rid of the impact of the past; it is still in his power to prevent the actions of the past from conditioning by their repercussions the actions of the present.[18]

What is in the mind of the wrongdoer, says Panikkar, is not 'the feeling of having done something intrinsically wrong, of having betrayed the confidence of the gods or broken a human pact; it is rather fear, fear of incurring punishment, fear of having set in motion a negative movement in the world, of having to go on living with a broken piece or a defective element.'[19] This fear characteristically issues in a denial of responsibility for what has happened. The novelist V. S. Naipaul, attempting to understand the land of his ancestors, quotes from a contemporary Indian novel in which a holy man, leader of a brahmin brotherhood, makes love in a moment of personal crisis to a woman from the untouchable class. The holy man feels that it was

> a moment that brought into being what never was and then itself went out of being. Formless before, formless after. In between, the embodiment, the moment. Which means I'm absolutely not responsible for making love to her. Not responsible for that moment. But the moment altered me – why?[20]

In the West, however, the acknowledgement of responsibility for one's deeds has deep roots in the Christian practice of repentance and confession. Perhaps the most remarkable demonstration of this lies in the fact that of the 2 million or more cases dealt with annually in the British criminal courts well over 90 per cent end with a plea of guilty by the defendant. Confession is perceived as good, if not for the soul, at least for ameliorating the sentence. 'Most suspects make admissions, confessions or statements in the police station thinking that this is in their best interests.' So it proves to be, if they continue by pleading guilty at the trial. 'The advantage is a lower sentence partly because the charge has often been reduced but also because the principle is firmly established by the Court of Appeal that a guilty plea normally entitles the defendant to a sentence discount of between a quarter and a third.'[21] Professor Zander's article on what has become known as 'plea bargaining' did not speculate on the origins of the custom. Clearly there are advantages to all parties, and indeed any significant increase in the number of contested cases over the present 10 per cent or less would produce intolerable congestion and delays in court proceedings. The tradition, however, surely owes something to the earlier church courts, and the principle there that penitence and confession were of themselves beneficial, leading to the restoration of the broken relationship between the sinner and his God, but also to the healing of that between the offender and his community.

This practice of plea bargaining implies that, at least in minor offences, what is at stake is not really the 'majesty of the law', but the protection of the community and the restoration of the offender to it, so that each can feel at home with the other. One might adapt the words of Jesus about the sabbath and say that 'the law was made for man, not man for the law'.[22] Nevertheless we cannot go further and say that man makes laws to suit himself. Whereas that may be true in small particulars we have seen that the sense of wrongdoing itself and the whole attitude of a society to it has deep religious roots and depends fundamentally on a people's cosmology – their whole understanding of the universe in which they live. What does this mean for a society in which people hold a

whole variety of religious beliefs, with widely different understandings of morality and law in consequence? Lord Devlin
has given one forthright answer to the problem in talking
about monogamous marriage. 'It has got there because it is
Christian, but it remains there because it is built into the
house in which we live and could not be removed without
bringing it down.'[23] In a similar way, though at a much more
superficial level, we have seen how the personal acknowledgement of wrongdoing has become written into the custom of
plea bargaining, without which the courts would find it
extremely difficult to function.

This should not lead us to suppose, however, that Westerners have nothing to learn from the moral concerns of the
rest of the world. Many in our Western world hold developed
and articulate views about social morality, racism, sexism, the
injustices connived at by capitalism, and other large-scale
issues. But some of the same people, in their personal lives,
settle for a morality which takes pleasure in flouting social
convention in the name of personal authenticity and moral
autonomy. It seems to such people pointless and fainthearted
to wish to fence the bounds of daily care and commitment to
one's sexual partner by anything so formal as a ceremony of
marriage. 'What', they ask, 'can mere formalities add to the
inward commitment we already have to each other?' The
social bonds and obligations, so sharply focussed in one
context, are dismissed as irrelevant in another. Similarly, at
the other end of the political spectrum, some of those most
vociferous about the breakdown of family life, abortion, video
porn and the growth of crime, are determined to secure their
freedom to improve their standard of living without the
restraints of considering the needs of society as a whole, and
the special needs of the sick, the poor, the handicapped and
the deprived, except as the whims of charity dictate.

In a world grown so small that is a dangerous as well as an
immoral doctrine. As Niebuhr wrote more than fifty years
ago: 'We can no longer buy the highest satisfactions of the
individual life at the expense of social injustice. We cannot
build our individual ladders to heaven and leave the total
human enterprise unredeemed of its excesses and corruptions.'[24] Niebuhr's prescription is the generation of a 'sublime

madness in the soul', a passion for justice on earth which is shorn of all illusions about achieving it. Habgood, quoting Dorothy Emmet, talks more prosaically of 'openness to a possibility which cannot be fully satisfied', a 'liberty of spirit' which is grounded in the 'transcendence of the Good'.[25] Whether we aim for a madness in the soul or a liberty of spirit it seems to me that the kind of mixed society we are now willy-nilly involved in is going to depend very heavily for its moral and spiritual health on those people in it who know themselves forgiven. We need people who can look at all our pasts, personal and collective, without flinching, because they know that the past can be robbed of its power to damage the future, and that because we can be released from that burden we can be free to share in the creation of a new world.

Chapter Eight

Work and Achievement

'The day is short, the work is great, and the labourers are sluggish, and the wages are high, and the Master of the House is insistent. It is not your duty to finish the work, but you are not free to neglect it.'
Rabbi Tarphon, first century CE[1]

'Most of us have jobs that are too small for our spirit.'
Contemporary professional worker[2]

Work has changed, and is about to change dramatically. It has been calculated that at the beginning of the eighteenth century, 92 per cent of the labour force worked as farmers to feed the other 8 per cent. Today it takes only 2 or 3 per cent to feed the rest. That process is still going on, and the early years of the next century – some predict – may see only 10 per cent of the labour force required to provide us with all our material needs – food, clothing, textiles, furnishings, houses themselves, and every kind of appliance and vehicle.[3] The impact of high technology, the 'mighty micro-chip', is only beginning to make itself felt, but is already ensuring that in most of our traditional industries the only profitable enterprises are those which can, in the bland current phrase, 'shed surplus labour', or in harsher terms, make workers redundant. Not only in the factory but equally in the office computer technology is beginning to dispossess thousands of workers of jobs which had been regarded as secure for decades if not for generations.

The future, as someone said, is not what it was. With such radical changes in the age-old patterns of productivity there must come massive changes in our whole understanding of and attitude to work. For well over 3 million people in Britain, and for corresponding numbers in other countries, change takes the painful and for some the permanent form of unemployment. Some try to reassure us with the promise that, as in the past, new machines will eventually create more jobs than they destroy, but most of those who have looked hard into the future are convinced that machines will inevitably reduce the number of people absolutely required to be involved in the processes of producing essential goods and services to a fraction of those so engaged now.[4] With the loss of jobs goes the traditional assumption of the value of work – the work ethic – to be replaced by a sense of bewilderment and failure.

What is this work ethic, and why is its redundancy so bewildering? It has often been called the 'Protestant Work Ethic'. Many commentators trace our current attitudes to work back to the Protestant Reformers, Luther and Calvin, and believe they were given their present shape during the English Industrial Revolution, beginning around 1760. Those who have drunk deep from Max Weber and R. H. Tawney may be surprised to read the quotation from a first century Jewish rabbi at the beginning of this chapter, and to listen to Rabbi Lionel Blue describing the Jewish attitude to work. Written in the days of relatively abundant employment in 1975, the second chapter of Blue's book on 'the Jewish path to God' is entitled 'Earning a Living in the Cosmos'. In his wise and witty way the author insists that Jews are irreversibly committed to being 'the holy company of righteous business-men, the pious organisers of communities, the committee men. . . the heroes who attend to the details of the world, and keep it going, for it does not go round by itself'. He speaks of the 'holiness of work' for the Jew, and recalls with a shudder the sign the Nazis hung at the entrance to the concentration camps – 'Work Makes Free' – so terrible 'because it distorted a truth which is one of the deepest in Jewish experience – the salvation to which daily work, honestly done, is the door.'[5]

In rabbinic fashion Blue speaks of God as our Employer rather than our Father, maintaining that God has given his people a task to do in this world, and that Jews live out their religious convictions by complete involvement in its affairs, rather than abandoning it for the contemplation of the world to come. Far from being other-worldly Jews are to find delight and salvation through being absorbed in the work their Employer has set them, though it must also be said that the best of that work is the study of *Torah*.[6] But then the Torah itself calls for energetic obedience to God in this world. 'Know also', said Rabbi Elazar, 'before whom thou toilest, and who the Employer is, who will pay thee the reward of thy labour.'[7]

In a revealing conclusion to this celebration of work, however, Blue admits that there is a crisis of purpose in modern Judaism. Work 'is used to meet God and evade Him at the same time. . . Work for Jews has a therapeutic function. . . to overcome fear and insecurity.' But 'a young Jewish generation released from the perpetual crisis which its elders endured. . . may have to go beyond work and law, and Israel, to an encounter with God.'[8] These are prophetic words, and not only for Jews and any modern crisis in Judaism that there may be. Not only Jews have misused work. We must return later to Blue's idea of going beyond work 'to an encounter with God'. David Bleakley also asks, 'Has the time come when the church must help society to transcend the work ethic?'[9] As he observes, the church comes late in the day to an interest in the subject, and some would feel that the church has actually forfeited its right to advise by its past collusion with the worst excesses of capitalism. But there have always been Christian voices which warned against enslaving whole generations of people in the factory and the mine, and in any case, if Christian teaching about work has been to any degree the problem, Christians should give a lead in re-thinking the whole question. E. F. Schumacher and others already have.

It seems to me that there are two related problems about the current significance of work in our lives, both of which are spotlit by the desolation of unemployment. One of these is the question of identity, and the other of achievement. In a highly mobile, technological society we tend most often to identify people by what they do rather than what they are. We 'place' people by their occupations, so that knowing what they do for a living is the key to understanding their likely educational and social background, their present and future financial and social status, and even their political ideology and general cast of mind. Inevitably, therefore, we want to know, within minutes of meeting a new acquaintance, not 'how do you do?' but 'what do you do?' The gradual erosion in Britain of class boundaries has only served to emphasize the significance of occupation in identifying people, since we can no longer assume an identity conveyed by birth.

At the beginning of the Protestant Reformation it was very different. Luther and Calvin and their followers were eager to assert the proper validity, in God's eyes, of every honest occupation. In the face of monasticism, with its implicit claim to be a higher way to salvation, they were determined to 'democratize' the Christian vocation and to enable the call to holiness to be answered *within* a multitude of secular employments. It was not necessary to shut oneself away from the world in order to do God's will, indeed that was likely – at least in Luther's experience – to lead only to spiritual pride alternating with a sense of futility and despair. What happened later was only the age-old confusion of means with ends. Just as monasticism, designed as a way of preserving the centrality of prayer within the church, became an end in itself, open to a thousand abuses, so, even more seriously, the Christian vocation to work in the world became fatally contaminated with the love of money and social prestige. Not that the Reformers were unaware of the danger. Though Luther and Calvin differed over the propriety of taking interest on commercial loans, both castigated excessive profit and the exploitation of the poor. Luther, socially much more conservative than Calvin, retained some of the medieval regard for poverty as an apostolic virtue. As capitalism developed, however, it was the characteristically Puritan virtues of thrift and industry which predominated. 'The Christian must conduct his business with a high seriousness, as in itself a kind of religion.'[10] In a passage made famous by Max Weber, John Wesley analyses the spiritual problems of the work ethic for his Methodist converts:

> I fear, wherever riches have increased, the essence of religion has decreased in the same proportion. Therefore I do not see how it is possible, in the nature of things, for any revival of true religion to continue long. For religion must necessarily produce both industry and frugality, and these cannot but produce riches. But as riches increase, so will pride, anger, and love of the world in all its branches. . . We ought not to prevent people from being diligent and frugal; we must exhort all Christians to gain all they can, and to save all they can; that is, in effect, to grow rich.[11]

The point of Wesley's final advice is that Christians should also give all they can to those in need, but the effect of the process he describes is neatly summarized by Weber in writing that 'the power of religious asceticism provided him (the bourgeois business man) with sober, conscientious, and unusually industrious workmen, who clung to their work as to a life purpose willed by God'.[12]

What happens, however, when 'a life purpose willed by God' is either so de-humanizing and 'soul-destroying' (a significant expression) as some mining and factory work has been and still is, or else there is no work? Here we begin to see the folly of defining people by the work they do, of referring to 'hands' or 'units of labour' instead of men and women. But more, we see the inadequacy of a theology, or ideology, which found all sense of purpose and achievement in the work which was necessary for daily bread. People began to live in order to work, instead of working in order to live. Work became a form of idolatry for many men, and for others a form of torture. Only the fortunate few with inherited incomes were in a position to live lives with a proper place for leisure and re-creation. Forgotten was the vision of the prophet, in which 'each man shall dwell under his own vine, under his own fig-tree, undisturbed'.[13]

Worst of all, the 'Protestant' work ethic became a highly individual thing, emphasizing competition rather than co-operation. As the older forms of energy – horses, wind-power, water-power – gave place to new, economic effort had to be systematized, for steam was most economically used in large units. The 'severer economic virtues', order, method, punc-tuality, system, regularity were increasingly required from a work-force whose skills needed to be more standardized, and interchangeable.

The change from a rural society where everyone knew each other to an impersonal urban mass was marked by the development of a new psychology based on competition and acquisitiveness. The misgivings of Luther and Wesley about wealth were forgotten. The Puritans spoke about pursuing 'some warrantable Calling for the publique good', but in an impersonal society the public good was easily set aside for private gain. Voices which challenged the new ethic of competitiveness provoked very sharp responses. David Bleakley quotes John Ruskin as a Victorian critic of the theory: 'Government and co-operation are in all things and eternally the laws of life. Anarchy and competition eternally and in all things, the laws of death.' A Manchester merchant hit back fiercely at Ruskin in *The Times*: 'If we do not crush him, his wild words will touch the springs of action in some hearts, and before we are aware, a moral floodgate may fly open and drown us all.'[14]

The necessity to make industry competitive is still being urged upon us in the 1980s, with the warning of dire consequences if we fail to do so. But the logic of competitiveness is that someone must go under. 'It's us or them.' This is why Ruskin called it 'the law of death'. If the ethic of competitiveness is examined in another sphere, such as sport, this becomes even more clear. Jonah Barrington, world-famous squash player, reflects on the need for a champion athlete

to have this deep, almost maniacal, hatred of being beaten. Ideally he must learn to control it, but he has to feel it inside. It's pride, it's shame, it's a dread of being inferior. It's a throwback to more primitive times, when you had to be competitive in order to survive. . . Sport is an alternative to war. It may be more civilised than actual warfare but the two are none the less analogous. . . Sport at the highest level is absolutely brutal. The fun element is negligible. For the people involved, sport is the survival area. Sportsmen are actually militants. We're peacetime soldiers. . . Losing is shame, despair and frustration.[15]

Some will no doubt dismiss this account of international sport – latter-day Roman gladiators in the arena – as exaggerated. Barrington admits to a degree of paranoia. 'They *are* out to get you!' However the combination of psychological and economic pressures on top sportsmen cannot be dismissed too lightly. Often a great deal of money is at stake in one man's will to win. The contrast with sporting behaviour developed in another culture, with a different valuation on competitiveness, is sometimes sharp and illuminating. Western players and followers of table tennis have frequently been puzzled by the Chinese attitude to the game. Table tennis in China is a national game played by millions daily, and their top players have easily dominated world championships. Nevertheless they appear to have allowed Japanese players to win certain events in some years, and in others they themselves have taken every place in the finals and then ensured that each top player won a single gold medal. A *Times* report expresses the Western bewilderment:

> It is not, as Westerners sometimes suppose, that the Chinese are totally opposed to individual competition. They compete too well, when they need to, for that. They believe in competition for self improvement and the passing on of skills to others. *But they do not make it their highest value.* Sometimes they prefer to display friendship to certain countries and towards each other. That understandably annoys the West and unfortunately their values and ours still seem too far apart to permit more than the vaguest communication.[16] (my italics)

It seems to me that if 'competition' is used for 'the passing on of skills to others', it might equally well be called 'co-operation', but Westerners see that as inimical to true sport. Barrington rejects the whole idea of the 'Inner Game' as the disinterested approach to sports performance, insisting that 'the natural, normal instinct *is* to compete, to overcome the opposition.'[17] Those who have been schooled in certain forms of Buddhism might well agree that competition is instinctive, yet go on to assert that that instinct must be eliminated, for it is actually the major obstacle to superlative performance. In language which rings strangely in Western ears we read that the sportsman must become 'purposeless and egoless. He must be taught to be detached not only from his opponent but from himself. He must pass through the stage he is still at and leave it behind him for good, even at the risk of irretrievable failure.'[18] In the Inner Game you are essentially competing against yourself, and the sport, whether archery or basketball, is only the medium for a much more fundamental endeavour. In this passage from *Enlightenment Through the Art of Basketball*, the pupil of the master basketball player Ogawa asks: What did Matsuoka learn?

> Ogawa answered: He was originally passionate to learn how to get the ball into the net quickly and easily. After ten days he had managed to control his temper. After twenty days he had lost his impatience. After thirty days he was shedding the desire to get the ball into the net. After fifty-five days he offered me the ball and left.[19]

It may seem that this excursus into sport has little to do with the serious subject of work. But the point is that central to both is some sense of achievement.

> Yanagi said: He has abandoned the art of basketball, but it
> seems that he has attained enlightenment as a male nurse
> Ogawa replied: That, too, is basketball.[20]

Is Zen Buddhism reminding us here of something we have forgotten, something overlaid in the Western scramble for wealth and position, a more inward reward for our labour? David Bleakley quotes an unemployed miner:

> Although there may be thousands of different kinds of jobs, as I see it, there are basically only two kinds of work. One is the sort that in the main is done for its own sake. Attached to it there are no notions of bosses or clocks or profits or wages and usually it is rewarding in itself. The other sort is that which is normally done in return for a weekly wage at docks, in factories, on building sites, down pits where one is a slave to time-keeping, norms, incentives, procedures, to say nothing of a whole clutch of rubbishy intangibles such as getting ahead and status and all the rest of the carrot spiel with which we have been well and truly brain-washed.[21]

We may ask whether it can ever be possible for everyone to have work which is 'rewarding in itself'. It is true that the micro-chip revolution promises to produce machines which will take on much of the slave labour which up to now has been done by human beings, but it is doubtful whether drudgery can be eliminated altogether. Provided security and satisfaction can be found in other ways it seems that there would be nothing but gain in the elimination of certain jobs like coal-mining, which are dirty, dangerous, and damaging to health, and the replacement of people by machinery. But in other jobs, like the care of small children, there may also be a good deal of back-breaking tedium, which cannot be so easily eliminated. People may be sustained in these jobs in different ways – the miners by a strong sense of solidarity and corporate identity – the much more isolated mother by her pride and hopes in her children. What there must be is some sense of purpose and value in the job itself.

If it has ever been necessary to prove that, it was proved by the Nazis. One of the survivors of Auschwitz describes how the prisoners had been compelled to take part in an 'experiment in mental health'. This consisted in moving sand from one end of a factory to another. It took some hundred people several hours to do, but when the job was completed they were told to take the sand back again to the original spot. The same orders were repeated day after day and week after week, until in the face of such meaningless toil people's minds began to give way. 'My comrades', writes the survivor, 'had died not at the hands of the Gestapo, but because they had nothing to live for and had been forced to do futile acts which killed their spirit.'[22]

How do we find an adequate and not a pathological purpose for our work and our effort? If we reject Jonah Barrington's excessive competitiveness – the *Observer* extract from his autobiography was entitled 'Murder in the Squash Court' – does the Eastern emphasis on detachment hold out more promise?

Yanagi enquired: What can you teach?

Ogawa answered: I can teach the art of holding on to the ball, and the art of letting it go. But only you can learn the art of not needing it.[23]

It may seem that here we have a philosophy totally opposed to the world-affirming traditions of the West, and especially to its Protestant, activist, makers and shapers. Yet we have heard Wesley on the danger of riches to religion, the riches that were the inevitable consequence of honest effort. A hundred years before Wesley the New England Puritan John Cotton had seen the same danger and called for something not unlike Hindu-Buddhist detachment:

There is another combination of vertues strangely mixed in every lively holy Christian, And that is, Diligence in worldly business, and yet deadness to the world. . . For a man to (take) all opportunities to be doing something, early and late, and loseth no opportunity, to go any way and bestir himselfe for profit, this will he doe most diligently in his calling; And yet bee a man dead-hearted to the world. . . though hee labour most diligently in his calling, yet his heart is not set upon these things, he can tell what to doe with his estate when he hath got it.[24]

'Yet his heart is not set upon these things' – 'Only you can learn the art of not needing it.' For an older Japanese Buddhist, Suzuki Shosan (1579–1655), the starting-point was the traditional Buddhist detachment from the world, but to this basic disengagement was added an energetic engagement with it for the sake of 'Heaven'. For Shosan, contemporary with the New England Puritans, and acquainted with Christianity only through the reports of Roman Catholic missionary teaching, 'Heaven' seems to have meant the 'general natural-moral order of the universe'. For him

farm work itself is Buddha-action. Only when your purposes are evil is it mean and shameful. . . For you to have been born a farmer is to have received from Heaven an official appointment to be one who nurtures the world. Therefore earnestly and with reverence entrust this body of yours to the way of Heaven. Do not concern yourself even momentarily with your body's welfare. Perform your work as a public service in the Righteous Way of Heaven.

Here is an East Asian Puritanism, it seems, which taught the same kind of engagement and the same kind of disengagement with the world. Shosan's paradox expresses it neatly:

those who support and establish the world are the very ones who give up the world[25]

A similar, but far better known understanding of work and ethics comes from the *Bhagavad Gita* and was popularized by Gandhi. Known as the doctrine of disinterested action (*niskama karma* or *naiskarmya*), it is preached consistently in the *Gita* as the answer to the dilemma of Arjuna, who faces the necessity of fighting in a civil war against his own relatives. He is told to perform his duty without desiring the consequences. 'Do the job that is incumbent on you, as a religious act.' But the word 'religious' here means 'renouncing the fruits of the action'. 'Seek to perform your duty', said the Blessed Lord (Krishna), 'but lay not claim to its fruits.'[26] This is an action-centred religious outlook, which hopes to evade all the ambiguities and corruptions in the soul which result from investing emotional capital in the outcome of one's actions. Gandhi expresses it in a very attractive way:

If we aspire to be good, we must ceaselessly work to serve others, serve them in a perfectly disinterested spirit. We should not serve anyone with the hope that he, too, will serve us one day, but we may serve him because the Lord dwells in him and we serve the Lord. If we hear anyone crying in distress for help, we should immediately run to him and help him. We should help the Lord crying in distress. After doing what was needed, we should feel that it was all a dream. Would the Lord ever cry in distress? In this way, all our acts of service will seem to us as dreams.[27]

Christians will be reminded here of Jesus' teaching in Matthew's Gospel about those who gave food and drink and clothing to the Lord, and ask 'when did we do these things?'[28] Attention has usually focussed on the Christ who is hidden in the person of the needy, but it may be that an equally important lesson lies in the unself-conscious goodness of those who do the giving. This is certainly the point of another of Jesus' sayings which is reminiscent here: 'When you do some act of charity, do not let your left hand know what your right is doing.'[29] Is the *Gita* saying the same thing: 'Work alone is thy proper business, Never the fruits it may produce.'?[30]

There are of course profound philosophical and theological differences between the *Gita* and Gandhi and Suzuki Shosan and Japanese Buddhism on the one hand and the biblical assumptions about creation and judgement which Christians share with Jews and Muslims on the other. The detachment called for is certainly of a different kind, depending on whether you regard this world as made by a good Creator who is determined to restore the work of his hands to its original goodness and beauty, or whether, with Hindu and Buddhist traditions, you see it as something which, with all its fleeting beauty, has neither beginning nor end nor purpose, and *from* which you escape into salvation. Moreover, it may be argued that neither Shosan in the seventeenth century nor Ogawa in this has greatly affected Japanese working life. Nirad Chaudhuri, among others, claims that the *Gita*'s doctrine of disinterested action is novel in Hinduism, was actually drawn from Stoicism, and in spite of Gandhi's advocacy has not taken root in India.[31] That may be true, but as we have seen, Christian thought about human work and action has been subject to similar corruption and neglect. The point, rather, is how we may arrive at an understanding of work and activity which will provide us with a way of living creatively in our present and imminent crises of work.

I have referred to the biblical doctrine of creation. Jews, Christians and Muslims each in their own way regard work and worship as inseparable, for is not the world the work of God, and are we not called to offer to him the work of our hands, as his employees, or stewards or servants? The Hebrew word *avodah*, the Arabic ʻ*ibādah* and the English *service* each carries the double meaning of work and worship, though they are used slightly differently. All that God requires from us by way of action, whether expressed in the 613 commandments of Judaism or the classical law of Islam, or the Christian concept of vocation, may be thought of either as work or as worship. Jews have traditionally seen the study of the Torah as the best of work, to be done particularly on the sabbath. The different labour of the rest of the week makes possible the joy of sabbath study, and if that work can be curtailed in favour of more study, so much the better.[32] Similarly the Christian monastic tradition, as expressed in the rule of St Benedict, prescribes both fixed times for manual labour and fixed times for sacred reading:

> But if the needs of the place or poverty demand that they labour at the harvest, they shall not grieve at this: for then they are truly monks if they live by the labours of their hands; as did also our fathers and the apostles.[33]

At this point I want to return to Lionel Blue's demand that we go 'beyond work and law, and Israel, to an encounter with God'. The saying from Rabbi Tarphon quoted at the head of this chapter continues in this way: 'Faithful is your Employer to pay you the reward of your labours.' But what will that reward be?

Jesus told a parable about the kingdom of heaven which can only be described as subversive. Free men are hired from the pool of those waiting for work at the time of the grape harvest. The fact that they have no vines of their own to work at suggests that they will be entirely dependent on the day's wages which, by Jewish law, must be paid to them at sunset. The normal wage is agreed upon. But the landowner, either because the vintage is particularly abundant, or the workers are slow, or he is sorry for the unemployed, goes back three times to hire more workers from the same pool, promising them 'a fair wage'. He specifically asks the final group, hired for only an hour, why they have been idle all day, and is told that there are no other employers ready to take them. When the men are paid off, it is in the reverse order to their hiring, but everyone is paid the full day's wage. This produces complaints from those who have worked the whole day, who expected some differential to distinguish them from those who had only worked for an hour. The employer reminds them of the contract, and his right to do what he likes with his own money, and ends by appealing to their generosity.[34]

The parable has been called the Parable of the Labourers in the Vineyard, and also the Parable of the Eccentric Employer. There can be little doubt that the landowner represents God, and equally that he does not behave according to normal commercial practice! The story comes after Jesus' unsuccessful appeal to a rich young man to abandon his wealth and follow him; Jesus' consequent warning to his surprised disciples about the spiritual danger of riches; and his apparent assurance of a special status and reward for them and other followers 'in the world that is to be'.

Like other parables, this one puzzles because of its disturbing unfairness. An everyday situation is given a sudden twist which shocks us into thought. The usual interpretation is that the story is another rebuke to those who protest against the opening of the kingdom of God to the undeserving. It could be a warning to his disciples not to seek for differential status among themselves, as he will soon have to say plainly.[35] It may be a sharp reminder that in God's eyes we are all servants: 'When you have carried out all your orders, you should say, "We are servants and deserve no credit; we have only done our duty."'[36] Jesus may even have the rich young man still in mind, and be illustrating the true riches of a generous heart compared to the cramped self-seeking of those who demand more than their due, just because others are given the same.

All these may be valid ways to read this parable, yet I believe that in a time of mass unemployment we are bound to look at it differently. Now what strikes us is the privilege of work compared to the boredom and frustration of having to stand around all day with nothing to do. The action of the employer not only rescues them from idleness and penury, but the way that he pays them off first seems to suggest that he wants to restore their morale and self-respect. He could have made his payment to them much more quietly and discreetly after the others had gone. This way ensured that they knew about it immediately. It sparked off an argument, but it also made public his concern for the latecomers, and helped them to hold up their heads. Surely the story is also saying to us that it is not the actual amount of work put in that matters, but the basic willingness to be useful. They wanted to work but no one wanted them. If they had not wanted to work, why come to the market-place?

With our contemporary experience of unemployment it seems very harsh to see these men as representing the undeserving and the immoral – the prostitutes and the tax-collectors. Or is that in fact how, after so many centuries of the work ethic, we do actually treat the unemployed? As David Bleakley points out, the regulations over supplementary benefit and part-time working among the unemployed still assume that full employment is the norm, and that anyone out of work for more than a year does not really want to work.[37] Yet those with inherited wealth, not to mention those on scholarships and grants of all kinds, have long received money for 'doing nothing'.

Jesus subverts the moral complacency which puts us above others in our own eyes, and goads us to rethink our conventional ideas of moral behaviour, and here, of work. In Western Protestant circles we have often preached against justification by works, but practised self-justification by Work. The great need of the day – and perhaps for the rest of this century – is to develop work which people can feel proud and purposeful to do. As machines increasingly take over the tasks of production such work will be more and more forms of service for other people, whether it is processing information or caring directly for people. Individualistic competitiveness will have to go. Market forces must make way for mutual co-operation. It will not be easy 'renouncing the fruits – the traditional rewards –of our actions', but as Rabbi Tarphon says, 'know that the reward of the righteous is in the time to come.' The apostle

Paul agrees: 'Work for the Lord always, work without limit, since you know that in the Lord your labour cannot be lost.'[38]

Chapter Nine

Freedom and Truth
in the Media

'I'm with you on the free Press: it's the newspapers I can't stand.'
Tom Stoppard

It is hardly possible to overestimate the influence of the mass media in shaping our understanding of contemporary events. On any given day about 60 per cent of the adult population of the United Kingdom hear or see at least one broadcast news bulletin.[1] Here is a massive responsibility on those who interpret the news to so many. And they are fewer than they were, for in the Western world newspapers have generally declined in number, and are owned by fewer people than at the beginning of this century.[2] As modern technology has made possible the rapid, even instantaneous, transmission of news from one side of the world to the other, the organization and expense involved has effectively concentrated the decisions about what is newsworthy into a relatively small number of hands. The sheer volume of raw material for news has increased to the point where the selection of appropriate items and their presentation are vital for maintaining circulation or audience. Consequently decisions about them are made within a given style and at the highest executive level. Here is immense power. How is it exercised?

A former journalist with *Time* magazine[3] describes how the weekly paper is put together. Editors receive story suggestions from reporters in *Time*'s thirty bureaux around the world, and construct a 'story list'. Reporters of the stories selected are then sent 'queries', sets of questions, sometimes quite elaborate, which indicate how the editors want the story reported. During the week editors and researchers check the facts and rewrite the material which the reporters send in. 'The bias in any *Time* story begins with the query. From the moment it is sent out, the shape of the story has been established.' Another *Time* journalist says 'The nuances of politics, the unconventional perspective, the diversity of opinion are left out because they present problems. It's always easier to fit things to what you think the top editors will want.' But what do they want?

Many people of left-wing political views point to the business connections of newspaper owners, and to the influence of advertizers on commercial television, and smell a conspiracy to present only such news as the 'military and industrial establishment' want people to hear. It is certainly not difficult to construct a case against the media for purveying primarily those facts and opinions which people in positions of power and influence want to be heard. The supposedly neutral British Broadcasting Corporation has from the beginning been a national institution responsible to, though not controlled by, the government of the day, and in times of crisis that is bound to show. Its first director-general, John (later Lord) Reith, wrote of the 1926 General Strike that 'since the Government in this crisis were acting for the people, the BBC was for the Government in the crisis too.'[4] At the height of the crisis itself he wrote that the Cabinet 'want to be able to say that they did not commandeer us, but they know that they can trust us not to be really impartial.'[5] But many people would think that impartiality was essential to news bulletins.

1926 is a long time ago, but there are those who reckon that the attitudes of Lord Reith are still dominant. The truth is probably more complex. So far from there being a conspiracy to maintain the 'establishment' view of events it may well be that the powerful constraints of time and money, imagination and experience, combine to present the news in a manner which makes most of it *recognizable*. Those news items which do not fall into the normal categories of news stories are usually the odd, curious, 'well, did-you-ever', pieces of eccentricity which confirm rather than threaten the reader or viewer's sense of what is normal. As C. Wright Mills, the American sociologist, wrote: 'Men live in second-hand worlds.' We depend for our understanding of what is going on in the world on people who themselves are busy recasting world events into packages that they and we will find basically familiar.

To write such things is to risk the accusation of cynicism or

worse. Yet the fact is that the objectivity which we have
assumed to be an integral part of our media peoples' profes-
sion is now seen to be an ever-receding goal – often sought but
never attained. Altaf Gauhar, at one time chief editor of
Karachi's *Dawn*, puts it in terms of the necessity of credibility:

> Naturally the agents of the mass media like to imagine
> themselves as agents of truth but the limitations of the mass
> media are always diminishing their pretentions. They can-
> not but be topical and interesting to remain in print. They
> talk of truth but the god they serve is the god of credibility.
> Media truth has to be credible – it must have the right
> 'intro' and the right 'peg' before it becomes readable or
> gains acceptance . . . Truth can survive without an audi-
> ence. Mass media cannot, hence the imperative of
> credibility.[6]

Gauhar's essay reprints for us the full text of the Declaration
on the Mass Media adopted by UNESCO in November 1978.
Time and again the statement reiterates the need for unpre-
judiced, objective reporting. The preamble refers to 'the
unrestricted pursuit of objective truth', to 'the moral obligation to seek the facts without prejudice'. Article II states that
'access by the public to information should be guaranteed by
the diversity of the sources and means of information available
to it, *thus enabling each individual to check the accuracy of facts and to
appraise events objectively*'[7] (my italics). But the trouble is that
'objectivity' and 'the accuracy of facts' are not the same thing.
It is not only the accuracy but the selection of facts which
matters. Which facts do matter? John Tirman, the former
Time magazine journalist already quoted, alleges that *Time's*
scrupulous attention to the minutiae of the spelling of names,
checking of figures and quotations, enables the magazine to
appear more authoritative than it really is. What has been
created, in his opinion, is a 'spurious air of insider's authority
buttressed by an endless stream of insignificant details'.[8]
Accurate trivia shore up wrong conclusions. Without sup-
porting his indictment of *Time*, we can see how that might well
happen to the best-intentioned of media presentations.

What is 'objectivity' and can it ever be achieved? A very
philosophical question perhaps, so in case anyone thinks it out
of place in a book about religious pluralism, let us take a case-

study of modern journalism. Third World nations often complain about the slanted account of their affairs put about by Western media. A typical letter in the Pakistani newspaper *The Muslim* (2 May 1983) claimed 'We all know that the news which we hear through BBC has a propaganda slant but is sometimes based on truth.' The writer went on to attack the Pakistani mass media for telling the public so little of the truth that they had to rely on outside sources like the BBC for what was happening in Pakistan itself. In Lahore in December 1971, during the brief war between Pakistan and India, we found ourselves listening to Radio Pakistan, All-India Radio and the BBC World Service in a three-cornered attempt to find out what was going on. At the time the BBC seemed to us to be exceptionally cautious in simply repeating the varied allegations made by the Indian and Pakistani news media about the progress of the war, often with no further comment except to say that verification was not possible. Pakistani friends used to tell us with some glee that in the previous war of 1965 the BBC had announced the fall of Lahore to Indian forces when in fact those forces had been halted a few miles from the city. Either the BBC had learnt discretion in dealing with news reports from the sub-continent or it was very conscious of the inevitable limitations of its one permanent reporter there.

How slanted or distorted is Western reporting about the Third World – or should we call it the South?[9] The case-study I want to pursue is Western reporting on Iran. Iran is certainly not one of the poorer nations of the South, and it has been the subject of massive Western attention during this century, yet it remains curiously unknown. Many Americans, it is claimed, identify Iran as an Arab country, and so the recipient of the classic stereotypes pinned on Arabs. The magazine *Arabia*, published in Britain by the Islamic Press Agency, describes these as 'traditional romantic elements of lustful desert dwellers dressed in flowing robes . . . tempered by the more sinister aspect of the intolerant and cruel villain derived from the standard Foreign Legion films'. To these long-established Holywood features have been added 'images of cunning and greedy – but at the same time spendthrift – oil-barons', the demons of Opec.[10]

Even for those who do not confuse Iranians with Arabs, Iran appears to be located in an area where normal assumptions do not operate, emotional language is given full rein, and demonic forces are held, by some, to be in complete control. Nothing in what follows is intended to condone summary executions on a large scale, imprisonment without trial, looting and murder, or any of the other ills of revolutionary Iran – ills which have attended many other revolutions in East and West. The point of a focus on Iran is to observe the well-documented misperceptions of the Western media concerning the events in Iran immediately before and after the Revolution of 1978–79. I have no desire to exonerate the killers of the son of the Anglican bishop in Iran, Bahram Dehqani-Tafti, the other attacks on the people and property of that church, or the much more official and systematic persecution of the Baha'i community in Iran. The shock of these events has obscured the earlier failure of the Western media fully to appreciate what was happening in Iran, or to see it in terms other than those prescribed by Western material interests – in one word, oil.

Altaf Gauhar has analysed the reporting of the British journal the *Economist* on the crucial months in Iran between December 1978 and February 1979. In his understanding, benefiting of course from hindsight, 'the people of Iran were protesting against the monarchy and the apparatus which governed their lives. The Shah of Iran used whatever force he could to sustain his rule, but by December 1978 it had become clear that he had lost his authority.'[11] The *Economist* at the time saw the situation differently. On 9 December 1978 it forecast that 'a year later the Shah's Iran may be disintegrating'; on 16 December that 'the uprising against the Shah faces the West with what is potentially its worst crisis in 25 years. . . Iran is not just a major oil supplier. It has also been the major local protector of Western interests.' The West could 'afford to be more outspoken than it has yet been in stating its vital interest in Iran in its determination to uphold it.'

The January 1979 issues of the *Economist* continued to support the Shah as a great national leader, and the Iranian people as exhibiting 'ungrateful resentments'. True, the Shah 'had for the last fifteen of his thirty-seven years of rule gathered total power into his own hands', but that was 'for reasons of national rather than personal ambition'. In February Khomeini's arrival was 'the coming of an obdurate Messiah'. On 24 February the *Economist's* verdict was that Khomeini had succeeded because the Iranian army suffered from certain structural weaknesses. The armed forces were not allowed to act effectively in time. They were confused, then paralysed 'when the Shah and his American advisers held them back from seizing power in the period when the Shah was visibly teetering'.

Gauhar's analysis is neatly summarized by the judgement of the *Columbia Journalism Review* on the parallel American treatment:

> By and large the American news media routinely have characterized the Iranian conflict as the work of turbaned religious zealots in league with opportunistic Marxists rather than – as they might have – the reaction of people outraged by a repressive regime. By doing so, the press has helped to misinform American public opinion and narrowed the range of debate on this bellwether foreign policy crisis.

Iranians themselves were perfectly clear, even if it was not safe for them to say, what was happening in the last years of the Shah. The Anglican bishop in Iran, with every reason to regret the Revolution, writes with complete clarity:

> By the late 1970s oppression was universal in the country. There was no longer any doubt that we were living in a police state. The whole country was demanding freedom, and the church added its voice to those who condemned oppression. When the Revolution came, we welcomed it. But it was not long before we found that we had exchanged one form of oppression for another even more severe.[12]

Gauhar attributes the failings of the Western media over Iran to the inherent limitations of the mass media, and the cultural orientation of the Western journalists. As I see it, the two things are intimately connected, for, as already argued, the limitations of mass media in terms of time and space constrain the presenters of current events to make them basically *familiar*, or at any rate credible. Where a faraway country is concerned, and coverage scanty, there is simply not time to persuade the reader, listener or viewer of the truth of an unfamiliar case. Who would have supposed, in the twentieth-century West, that a people could rise against the sophisticated weaponry of a modern army and rid themselves of an unpopular ruler armed only with their bare hands and the belief that God would honour the justice of their cause? When the ruler happens to be a strong ally of the West, and the religious zeal that of Islam, the task of realigning the sympathies of Western audiences in the time available becomes herculean. Most journalists did not attempt it, or if they did, we can assume that their attempts were edited out.

A more extensive analysis than that of Altaf Gauhar has been carried out on the whole Western (especially American) perception of the Islamic world by Edward Said.[13] Said, it should be noted, is not a Muslim, nor a believer in any religion. A professor of English and Comparative Literature at Columbia University, Said has developed a close interest in the Western understanding of Islam and Muslim affairs as an example of what he calls 'the affiliation of knowledge with power'.[14] His thesis is that the contemporary study of Islam in Western, and especially American academic institutions is finally determined by Western foreign policy interests, and can have little claim to 'objectivity'. These academic scholars on Islam, known for many years as 'orientalists' are often prominent in media discussions about events in Muslim countries, lending their authority to the reports delivered there. Yet, claims Said:

> The hardest thing to get most academic experts on Islam to admit is that what they say and do as scholars is set in a profoundly and in some ways an offensively political context. Everything about the study of Islam in the contemporary West is saturated with political importance.[15]

At the beginning of the hostage crisis 300 reporters were in Tehran, yet there was not a single Persian-speaker among them. Iran had been cast by Western minds in the role of a state developing rapidly into a 'modern' society, a test case, even a show-case of 'modernization'. So led away, claims Said, were the observers of Iran by their own ideology of 'modernization' that they could only see the Shah as a casualty to 'fanaticism'. The words 'fanatic' and 'barbarism' recur endlessly throughout news reports on Islamic affairs, and especially on Iran, for no traditional Western school of thought finds an easy affinity with what they understand to be Islam. 'For the right, Islam represents barbarism; for the left, medieval theocracy; for the center, a kind of distasteful exoticism.'[16] Consequently the whole representation of the Muslim world becomes distorted in Western eyes: 'it is only a slight overstatement to say that Muslims and Arabs are essentially covered, discussed, apprehended, either as oil suppliers or as potential terrorists.'[17]

Said's book *Covering Islam* has pages of quotation from American press and media reporting on Iran which characterize Islam as marked by hatred of the West, as inimical to civilization, subject to the irrational frenzy of religious passion ('Islam amok'), and generally a menace to the West since 'wherever there has been murder, war, protracted conflict involving special horrors "Islam clearly played an important part".'[18] Said's conclusion is characteristically forthright, perhaps exaggerated, but nevertheless disturbing:

> I have not been able to discover any period in European or American history since the Middle Ages in which Islam was generally discussed or thought about *outside* a framework created by passion, prejudice and political interests. . . Orientalist scholars have tended to use their understanding as experts to deny – or sometimes even to cover – their deep-seated feelings about Islam with a language of authority whose purpose is to certify their 'objectivity' and 'scientific impartiality'.[19] (author's italics)

I began by noting that Said was not a Muslim. Now it must be observed that he is a Palestinian, from one of the Eastern Christian communities, though not himself a believer. This context may explain his sharp perception of Western pretensions to 'civilization', of the unconscious identification of Christianity and the American way of life, and the castigation of Islam and Muslim societies as 'backward', 'barbarous' and 'medieval'. For Christians of the Middle East not only regard themselves as the 'original' Christians, with a better title to Christian authenticity than any other cultural group. They are also conscious of having suffered deeply at the hands of Western Christians from the Crusades onwards. Whatever weaknesses they would admit to in the Eastern churches, they would also claim that these have been magnified and even deliberately exploited by French, Russian and British imperial adventures, by European and American missionaries in the nineteenth century, and by Western attempts to secure their oil supplies in the twentieth century. Every Western interference in Middle Eastern affairs is seen as a rerun of the Crusades, with all the anti-Muslim propaganda that ran riot in the Middle Ages.

In fact that propaganda is very much alive, as can be seen by such books as Marius Baar's *The Unholy War: Oil, Islam and Armageddon*[20] or Ishak Ibraham's *Black Gold and Holy War: The religious secret behind the petrodollar.*[21] Both books feature the Ayatollah Khomeini on their front cover, and amply illustrate Said's contention that Islam is seen principally in a political context, even by some of those who set out to write specifically for a Christian religious audience. Or is it simply that publishers and publicists generally find it impossible to turn down the potent combination of the rise to supreme authority (Khomeini), fall from it (the Shah), religion, war and apocalyptic vision?

I do not mean to imply, by any of this, that Iranians are scrupulously fair in their reports about the West. It is widely known that the current slogan for the United States in Iran has been 'the Great Satan'. The cartoons about President Carter in the Iranian press were quite as offensive as American cartoons about Khomeini, with the qualification that in general the Western press has not hesitated to ridicule Islam, by implication, along with Khomeini. So we see a picture of Muslims prostrate in their prayer ritual with the explanatory caption: 'They are all looking for the Ayatollah's contact lens!' I cannot imagine Muslims returning the gibe with a cartoon of a Western leader at the communion table, which would be a parallel case. For the East understands a religious motive, and the West does not. In Edward Said, despite his unbelief, we hear the authentic voice of the Eastern church, warning us not to take our Western culture as the measure of world affairs, particularly where they claim a religious inspiration.

Yet this is precisely what we have done, under the cover of seeking 'objectivity'. 'But', the retort may come, 'we naturally suppose our view of world affairs to be the right one; if we didn't, we wouldn't hold it! I assume that my view of the world is objectively true until someone convinces me I am wrong. Then I change it. Truth is not subject to democratic vote.' There are profound problems here, related partly with Said's theme of the 'affiliation of knowledge with power', but at a deeper level with the necessity of having some system of values for any perception to be possible of what is significant in the multitudinous events of the world about us.

Someone said 'Tell me who is asking the question, and I will tell you what the answer is.' We might, with a touch of cynicism, rephrase that to read, 'Tell me who is paying for the answer, and I will tell you what the question is.' Said has alerted us to the fact that the same American consultants on the Middle East serve their academic institutions, business corporations and also the United States government. He draws an interesting, and perhaps ominous parallel between the French and British orientalists of the last century, who prepared the intellectual ground for those countries' imperial adventures in the Middle East, and American scholars of today busy compiling information of great interest to the American government in its economic and foreign policy decisions. As a reviewer of Said's book wrote, 'Said squarely confronts American Middle East scholars with a question too many of them have heretofore ignored; at whose service shall their intellect be put?'[22]

But the relationship of knowledge and power is only one aspect of the deeper question about values. It is an important political question as I remember every time I am in the library of the Selly Oak Colleges and look at the shelf of books on South Africa – books donated by the South African government and carefully so marked. If we are, in C. Wright Mills' phrase, condemned to 'live in second-hand worlds', how can we make sure they are not in fact third- or fourth-hand? How can we pierce the mask of propaganda and reveal the unfamiliar face of the stranger behind the stereotype? It is always easier, of course, to recognize propaganda designed to express a different set of values from our own. It was reported in July 1981 that Pakistan's military government had directed newspapers not to carry crime and police reports on front and back pages. The government wanted to see the end of 'glorified crime reports' and criticism of police administration.[23] One view of such a report would be that the Pakistan government was clearly worried at the incidence of crime and wanted to remove potential fuel for its own unpopularity to less obvious places. But there may also have been a recognition that reporting can glamourize crime, and that if any publicity is good publicity criminals should not be allowed to benefit from it.

More significantly, it may well be that in an Islamic state like Pakistan, with a well-articulated ideology of its own, reports of criminal activities and police incompetence are simply not news. That is to say they do not fit easily into the image that the Islamic state has of itself. This is by no means straight hypocrisy. No one wishes to deny that these things happen, only that they should not be given over-much importance. Why allow them to drive the real achievements of the nation off the front page? How could it benefit the nation to become obsessed with such things? Countries such as Pakistan with limited means of mass education and communication inevitably want to control their national media and use them to foster positive nation-building ideas.

At a deeper level still lie the unspoken assumptions about human failure and sin. In Christian faith this is something to be brought out into the open and confessed with a full acknowledgement of responsibility. In Islam sin is rather a forgetfulness, a momentary blindness to the task of living God's way, to the human responsibility to be his servant. In his mercy God may overlook the error so we should not dwell on it. Is there even lurking there the idea that we might unwisely draw his attention to it?

What is news? Two history teachers long ago produced the classic tongue-in-cheek definition of their subject: 'History is not what you thought. It is what you can remember. All other history defeats itself.'[24] Insofar as news is contemporary history the same definition must apply. It is easy to launch into censorious attacks on the presentation of news, particularly on television, for providing more a form of entertainment than hard facts. Many people are aware of the danger of viewing the troubles of the world as a nightly spectacle to accompany their late-evening drink. Particularly when watching independent television news bulletins I have often winced at the juxtaposition of some advertizing trivia coming immediately after a harrowing scene of refugees or people filmed in the aftermath of some tragic accident. In addition, it is difficult to let go the suspicion that a number of items are selected for showing principally because they lend themselves well to visual presentation, while other equally or more important items are omitted because they do not.

But we have to face the fact that the presentation of news in print or electronically *is* a form of entertainment, or better, an art form. You have to persuade people to buy it, listen to it, watch it. It must be readable, or viewable, if not (as Sellar and Yeatman had it) 'memorable'. 'All other history defeats itself.' The comic touch, the acknowledgement of incongruity, is an important ingredient in our world-view, reminding us not to take ourselves too seriously. Life cannot be viewed wholly rationally, for there always lurks in some corner a pin to prick our pretensions and bring our grandiose dreams back to earth. The cartoonist or the wit who uses that pin is showing us how difficult it is to construct and articulate a scale of values which we can confidently assert to be of absolute worth. The humorist can almost always outflank us, by recalling the sense of a different proportion. So the jester and the prophet hold hands.

It may seem that this discussion of the media has come to extremely negative conclusions. I have suggested that the boasted 'objectivity' of Western media is shown up by close examination to be deeply compromised by the need to construct, under considerable pressures of space and time, a recognizable picture of the world. What is not easily recognizable is not ordinarily presented, and what is presented is clearly dependent upon deeply-held assumptions and values which are not often carefully scrutinized or even articulated. At the same time it may be doubted just how this could be adequately done. We are generally glad when someone describes their own standpoint, their political and religious convictions, the experiences which have moulded them, because that helps us to assess the significance of what they say next, and the authority it will hold for us. But no one can

completely and exhaustively analyse their own presuppositions, any more than they can examine their own retina.
There is no language to do it with, and no place to stand on
from which it can be done. We cannot be objective about our
own value-system.

Are we then condemned to flounder in a sea of relativism?
Can we say no more of any claim to truth than Mandy Rice-
Davies' famous remark from the witness-box: 'Well, he would
(say that), wouldn't he?' Perhaps the first lesson is that of
intellectual humility, that we must say very often that we do
not know. If a close attention to political history suggests that
there are no innocents, that every nation and class and
cultural group has skeletons in its cupboard, then perhaps it is
equally true that none of us see or report with unclouded
vision, that what religious people call 'sin' enters deeply into
the whole process of our perception of what goes on around us
in the world. Sin, as Jesus implied, is in the mind long before it
becomes an act.[25] Since the human past is loaded with
injustice and evil of every kind it would actually be surprising
if we were able to see the present clearly.

In itself, however, intellectual humility may lead us only to
despair, to the feeling that there is nothing we can accurately
report. Or it may turn to a prevailing cynicism, the occupa-
tional disease of the journalist who has seen endless misery go
unregarded and his own best stories spiked. In the Christian
understanding repentance – what here I have called 'intellectual humility' – always goes with faith and hope. What is
'faith' and 'hope' where the media are concerned? It is not, I
would suggest, a matter of reporting only 'positive' news, of
banishing all the world's woes from the front pages to make
way for some contrived 'good news', some wearisome daily
insistence that all is well in the best of all possible worlds. But
nor is it 'a tale told by an idiot, full of sound and fury,
signifying nothing'. The very attempt to record the happenings of the day presumes that the exercise is worthwhile, that
some significance, if we can but interpret it correctly, lies in
the things that human beings achieve and do to each other, for
good and for ill. We may make endless mistakes about their
true significance, but if events *have* a real significance then we
are no longer trapped in a totally impersonal world, where the

patterns of the stars at our birth determine our destiny.

Moreover, because of the speed and ease of communications, news services are actually growing. Information is so important that people complain of being saturated with news reports of various kinds. Here again, for all our failures at 'objectivity', the growing insistence that the *whole* story be told, that a story be covered from several angles, is actually a sign of hope. For the implication is that *all* people matter, that they all have a story to tell, and that it is worth our while to listen carefully to one another, even from one end of the earth to the other. Here is an affirmation that people – all people – are important, which may go some way to protect us from the tyrannies of those who are sure they know what is good for us.

So far what I have said could be said by any secular humanist. Where, as a Christian, I would go further is in the faith and hope of a God who is responsible for all the millions of men, women and children that the media report about, and who has never left us 'without some clue to his nature'.[26] The Christian, like the Jewish and Muslim, understanding of God, is of a God who is active in history, who not only sustains the whole universe he has created and keeps it continually in being, but who makes himself and his ways known to us. The prophets were men who were normally deeply involved in the public affairs of their time, and did not hesitate to comment on them under the influence of what they were convinced was God's direction. I believe that journalism today is essentially a prophetic role, searching in the maelstrom of events for the things that really matter, inevitably getting some things wrong, but continually reaching out for the transcendent word. For we were made to receive communication that is 'tongued with fire'. 'Man cannot live on bread alone; he lives on every word that God utters.'[27] But more than that, if the New Testament is to be believed God himself has become an event in human history and in Jesus of Nazareth we see God himself uniquely present. This is not an incarnation like the *avatars* of India whose humanity is so tenuous that they possess no shadow and their feet barely touch the ground,[28] but an immersion into the human lot of tears, sweat, blood and laughter. The good news of Christianity is the life of Jesus the Christ. Here is an event which sheds its light on all other events, which is the key that turns the lock of understanding on all that happens. Can we but look deep enough, we find at the heart of every human happening the form of the suffering, triumphant Lord. 'God was in Christ reconciling the world to himself.'[29]

Of course this is the language of faith. But I would contend that of all professions journalism, if it is to have any integrity, depends on faith of some sort, faith to sustain and inform the conviction that the job is worth doing. The question is: what sort of faith?

Chapter Ten

Wealth and Power

A Christian leader in Sri Lanka once told me, 'People think that all the trouble in the world is because of wealth. Some have too much and others have too little. But it isn't the sharing of wealth that is the problem; it is the sharing of power.' In his view, the possession of power led naturally to the possession of wealth, or the opportunity for it, so that the problem of power subsumed that of wealth. It was a memorable remark from the context of Sri Lanka, itself coveted in succession by Chinese, Portuguese, Dutch, French and British, and continually wracked by the struggle between Singhalese and Tamil.

The issues of wealth and power are of course inextricably linked, but it does seem to me that there is a fundamental moral problem involved in the exercise of power which does not belong to the mere possession of wealth in itself. Power might be defined as the ability to make decisions which have far-reaching implications for other people, and to make them with or without the consent of those people. When that consent is regularly dispensed with, and machinery evolved for making it unnecessary, we have arrived at what has been called 'institutional violence', the perpetuation by the ultimate sanction of force of decision-making by the few. The term 'institutional violence' is regarded rather dubiously by those who feel it has been invented to justify a corresponding 'revolutionary violence', but it does have the merit of pinpointing the 'bottom line' of all political decision-making, which is the ultimate threat of force. In the world as we know it no government can rely on the consent of all of the citizens all of the time, and therefore the use of force, of violence exercised on behalf of the national institution, can never be ruled out. This was made very clear in Britain by parliamentary answers to speculative questions about what would happen to women peace protesters who succeeded in penetrating the last defences of nuclear weapon installations. 'The soldiers have orders to open fire' was the answer, and it was not seriously challenged by any political party.

Leaving aside the particular issue of nuclear weapons, most people would probably admit that every state must be able to employ the ultimate sanction of force for the sake of its own security. At the same time it is abundantly clear from human history that it is extremely difficult to prevent the premature use of force long before that ultimate situation is reached, in the name of national or group 'security'. The situation quickly arises in which large masses of people have no effective say whatever in fundamental decisions concerning their own lives, because these are made by other people in the interests of 'security'. Attempts to express opposition are met speedily by forcible repression. This is the situation, in varying degrees, in most countries of the world. Even those that pride themselves on their 'democracy' and 'free speech' have to admit that the actual reins of power are normally controlled by comparatively few, and that the channels of communication for dissent are very limited.

This enforced silence, this fearful stifling of the voices of protest, is surely the fundamental problem of our world, and not poverty in itself. We know that it is possible to feed and educate the population of the world, if only there were a political will to do it. If a man can be put on the moon, the technical problems are not insoluble. The trouble is that the political will does not exist because the people in power are not personally affected by poverty, disease and ignorance, and those who are have no voice. How can 'the meek inherit the earth'?[1]

Christians believe that although this and other sayings of Jesus referred to the time of God's final judgement on the world, they have already begun to apply because of what God has done through Jesus. The Greek word *praeis* is variously translated as 'meek', 'humble', 'gentle', 'of a gentle spirit'. Can we really see any prospect of that attitude making any impression on the political life of the world? Is not this the real question of our times, and not the non-question of whether religion should be 'brought into' politics? (It is of course quite impossible to keep it out.) Is a heavenly faith of any earthly relevance? Or to phrase the same question differently, has religion in all its manifestations anything to offer for the solution of our basic world problems? What does religion have to say about power?

We will see that a good deal of contemporary religious writing is very concerned about power and the powerless, but first it may be necessary to clear away some misconceptions about the relationship between religion and political power. It is very tempting to argue from historical events, both remote and recent, to the effect that 'all the trouble in the world is caused by religion'. It is of course true that the religious instinct is a very powerful one, and strong convictions sometimes lead to extreme actions. But it could equally well be argued that religion is very often used as a legitimating argument for courses of action already decided on other grounds.

It is actually quite difficult for professional historians to decide when a genuinely religious motive has been uppermost or even what that might be. One might suppose that in the case of contemporary Islam at any rate, the religious motive would be plain. But at least one distinguished Muslim scholar and observer of contemporary politics would disagree. Mohammed Ayoob sees Islam as the religion par excellence of the Third World, and Muslim countries as sharing in the characteristic changes going on in Third World countries. He sees a rejection of imported models of development and a return to Islam-based politics as 'more because it is culturally indigenous rather than religion-oriented'. 'The political reassertion of the Muslim world symbolizes very well the general stirrings of discontent within the Third World against the present distribution of power within the international system'.[2] Seen in this way, leaders and policies as different as that of Nasser and Khomeini belong to one spectrum of Third World revolt against Western political domination. The revolt has an Islamic character because these are Muslim countries, but he implies that the basic movement at work is 'the Third World's aspiration for autonomy from the managers of the international system'.[3]

Western observers (Ayoob himself teaches in Australia) may raise eyebrows at such attempts to delink Islam and current Muslim politics, just as many from Muslim, Hindu or Buddhist societies would question sharply Western Christians who wanted to claim that the struggles going on in Northern Ireland or Central America were 'nothing to do with religion'. The fact is clearly that both religious and other motivation is at work. We can leave to the historian the task of 'discovering just what sorts of beliefs and practices support what sorts of faiths under what sorts of conditions'. At the same time we share his basic concern: 'Our problem, and it grows worse by the day, is not to define religion but to find it.'[4] If we may not look with too much confidence at our European history to see Christianity 'at work' in society,[5] and if detached modern observers find it similarly difficult to trace Islam unambiguously 'in action',[6] can we nevertheless find in religion somewhere the perceptions and the vision we need?

The Christian faith begins with repentance, as the first words of Jesus' public life make clear: 'Repent, and believe in the gospel.'[7] That repentance might well begin by acknowledging the collective folly of Western man in his exploitation of the resources of the world, and his subjugation of those less technically advanced than himself. The point is made with great poignancy in a letter from the Amerindian Chief Seattle to the then president of the United States in 1855:

We know that the white man does not understand our ways. One portion of the land is the same to him as the next for he is a stranger who comes in the night and takes from the land whatever he needs. The earth is not his brother but his enemy and when he has conquered it he moves on. . . His appetite will devour the earth and leave only a desert. The sight of your cities pains the eyes of the red man, but perhaps it is because the red man is a savage and does not understand. . .

We might understand if we knew what it was that the white man dreams. What hopes he describes to his children on long winter nights. What visions he burns into their minds so that they will wish for tomorrow. But we are savages. The white man's dreams are hidden from us.

The whites too shall pass, perhaps sooner than other tribes. Continue to contaminate your bed and you will one night suffocate in your own waste. When the buffalo are all slaughtered, the wild horses all tamed, where is the thicket? – gone. Where is the eagle? – gone. And what is it to say goodbye to the swift pony and the hunt? The end of living and the beginning of survival.[8]

Chief Seattle was bewildered at the proposal that land could be bought, as though anyone owned it. For him the point was that the earth belonged to God and was precious to him, and 'to harm the earth is to heap contempt on its creator.' He could not understand the desire the white man seemed to have to be free of God, 'exempt from the common destiny'.[9] The same thought comes from a very different source – the Shi'ite scholar Seyyed Hossein Nasr. 'Modern man has simply forgotten who he is'.

His only hope is to cease to be the rebellious creature he has become, to make peace with both Heaven and earth and to submit himself to the Divine. . . The missing dimension of the ecological debate is the role and nature of man himself and the spiritual transformation he must undergo if he is to solve the crisis he himself has precipitated.[10]

Western man has lost his way because he has tried to understand himself without reference to the God who made him. So argue these two witnesses, 120 years and worlds apart in culture and education. But is it possible that the problem of human beings exploiting one another and the world they live in should turn out in the end to be simply one of belief – belief in an omnipotent Creator? The agnostic may be excused for feeling that he has heard this before, and that the prescription seems to have made little desirable impact on human history so far.

I have referred above to the difficulties of deciding what is and what is not a religious motive in human events. It is very hazardous to try to prove anything about religion from history. It is more important to recall what is meant by 'belief'. When we speak about belief in God we are not primarily referring to an opinion about how the universe originated, how it is sustained and how it will end. We are talking about a personal relationship of obedience and trust to one who is ultimately responsible for all life, both in the sense that it derives from him and that he has not ceased to care for and control it. Our human accountability to him is simply a measure of the lesser responsibility he has delegated to us. We were made to delight in doing his will, being gardeners in his garden.

This is the teaching of the Bible, as it is the teaching of the Qu'ran and the instinctive understanding of many so-called 'primitive' people, of whom we may take Chief Seattle as a representative. We come from God and we return to him. As Chief Seattle wrote: 'One thing we know, that the white man may one day discover, our God is the same God. You may think that you own him as you wish to own our land, but you cannot.' Western man has announced his independence of God and tried to carry on as though God were not. In Bonhoeffer's famous words: 'Man has learned to cope with all questions of importance without recourse to God as a working hypothesis.'[11] But forty years on from Bonhoeffer we can see that the confidence he observed in Western secular man has been seriously eroded, and the words of men like Chief Seattle have come back to haunt us.

Bonhoeffer wanted to affirm the achievements of Western civilization and resist any attempt to drag human beings back into some kind of ecclesiastical tutelage. He objected to well-meaning religious people 'having as their objective the clearing of a space for religion in the world or against the world',[12] as though God could be given a reservation in which he could live his out-dated life, like the American Indians or African wild animals threatened with extinction.

If there is a God he has to be the total context of our lives, not some small minority concern within them. There are many who wish to confine our apprehension of God's demands to so-called 'ultimate questions', and resent the comments which religious leaders make about everyday public affairs. 'The business of the clergy is saving souls. Let them get on with that, and concentrate on filling their churches.' It is true that religious leaders' comments may be naïve or inadequately informed, or even unduly one-sided. But we cannot concede that God is concerned only with the private life of the individual and the saving of his 'soul'. We are public as well as private people, and no part of our lives, individual or corporate, can be hidden from his scrutiny or regarded as none of his business. Therefore we have to be concerned for his sake with the decisions that are taken in our name.

This long digression about the nature and scope of faith in

God in the contemporary world has been necessary to establish what kind of dimension is missing among those who exercise power in the world. It is simply one of accountability, not to any electorate, parliament or praesidium (though these are vital checks on individual delusions of grandeur) but to the God who is supremely responsible. Only such faith can hold in check the illusion of self-adequacy. The famous dictum of Lord Acton, that 'power tends to corrupt, and absolute power corrupts absolutely', has at its heart the recognition that those who make decisions on behalf of others easily come to have excessive confidence in their own powers of judgement. They feel adequate in themselves for what they have to do, without reference to any supreme authority. Muhammad attacked the merchants of Mecca for precisely this illusion that they were not accountable for what they did:

No indeed; surely Man waxes insolent,
for he thinks himself self-sufficient.
Surely unto thy Lord is the Returning.[13]

As Kenneth Cragg comments on this passage:

(Man) must insistently relate all circumstance, all achievement, all intention, to this heavenly authority. He is to refuse to 'presume', not only as to what lies in the uncertain disposition of eternity, but over what seems securely within his will and reach. He is to boast no adequacy about which he is not utterly reliant upon God and expectant only from Him.[14]

In both the Bible and the Qur'an the test of such accountability is the treatment by the powerful of the powerless, the poor, widows, orphans. The Qur'an recalls Muhammad's own experience at the hands of God and draws the obvious conclusion:

Did he not find thee an orphan, and shelter thee?
Did he not find thee erring, and guide thee:
Did he not find thee needy, and suffice thee?
As for the orphan, do not oppress him,
and as for the beggar, scold him not;
and as for thy Lord's blessing, declare it.[15]

In the New Testament the letter of James similarly sums up all the denunciations by the prophets of those who were careless or oppressive of the poor: 'The kind of religion which is without stain or fault in the sight of God our Father is this: to go to the help of orphans and widows in their distress and keep oneself untarnished by the world.'[16] Human beings are one race and one family under God, and therefore it is imperative that they care for each other, the stronger for the weaker. The fundamental test of human strength and maturity is whether the poor and the powerless are helped to become strong and mature themselves, just as the basic test of a family is whether it helps its children and its weaker members to grow big and strong. Caring for people is not a matter of maintaining them in their weakness (unless their handicap has absolutely no remedy), but of helping them to grow strong.

It is surely in this sense that God may be said to have a 'bias to the poor'.[17] It is not that God cares less for the rich than for the poor. (Often religious people have thought that he cared *more* for the rich, seeing their wealth as a sign of his special favour.) It is simply that the rich and the powerful are tested by their attitude to the poor and the weak. Amos declares that God is sickened by the worship of those who oppress the poor and crush the destitute:

Spare me the sound of your songs;
I cannot endure the music of your lutes.
Let justice roll on like a river
and righteousness like an ever-flowing stream.[18]

Jesus likewise says that whoever has fed the hungry, looked after strangers and needy people, and visited the sick and the prisoners, has done so for him, whether they knew it or not.[19] Conversely, if they have failed to do these things, they have failed to do them for him. It is difficult to read these passages and deny that there is a divine 'bias to the poor'.

In his book with that title David Sheppard, the Bishop of Liverpool, outlines from the British context what might be involved in beginning to redress the balance:

When I was first ordained and went to serve in inner city London, I would have said that people are the same wherever they live. I believed that if you could change individuals, that was the only way to change the world. I expected broadly to see the same response to the Gospel, to educational and career opportunities, whatever the context in which people lived. I've learned that there are massive blocks in the way of such responses for inner city people, whether they live in the inner city itself or in the vast corporation estates on the perimeter of a city. The Gospel needs to proclaim the need and the possibility for God *both* to change people from inside out *and* to change the course of events to set people free to make such choices.[20]

'Setting people free to make choices' for themselves, instead of being at the disposal of other people's choices is a programme for giving power to the powerless. It is important to recognize that this is not a new programme. For decades, if not for centuries, education has been a route through which many people have found an ability to make decisions for themselves, and to acquire the economic security which opened up a further range of choices. The trouble has been, both in countries like Britain and in all Third World countries, that education has invariably favoured a fortunate few who through a combination of circumstances and ability have been able to escape from a background of poverty themselves, but left that situation exactly as it was before. It may indeed have become marginally worse through the loss of a gifted member. Education has been an escape route, a ladder to individual but not community achievement, the channel for the international brain drain. When this happens on a large scale to, for example, particular areas of a big city, it creates what David Sheppard calls 'communities of the left behind,'[21] groups of people suffering from multiple deprivation.

There can be little doubt of how the Bible views the duties of the well-off towards the poor:

When your brother-Israelite is reduced to poverty and cannot support himself in the community, you shall assist him as you would an alien or a stranger, and he shall live with you. You shall not charge him interest on a loan, either by deducting it in advance from the capital sum, or by adding it on repayment. You shall fear your God, and your brother shall live with you.[22]

There is to be no exploitation of a man who has fallen on hard times, but genuine help, for the Israelites form one community under God – 'your brother shall live with you'. In modern cities, however, and in the international community, we acquiesce in a situation in which upwards of 6 million people in Britain live in a poverty trap which no government has cared to eliminate, and in which the international terms of trade have for thirty years been moving against the interests of the poorer developing countries.[23] Charles Elliott, the former director of Christian Aid, concludes that nationally and interna-tionally there is 'a systemic skew against those whose total social needs are greatest'. The poor, all over the world, are precisely those whose access to education, health care, and adequate housing and employment is systematically 'skewed'. This is particularly true for certain minorities, like the black and Asian people of Britain, for whom unemployment may be double or even three times the rate for all workers of the same age group.[24]

Relief organizations such as Oxfam and Christian Aid have brought home to us in recent years the scale of world poverty, and tried in dozens of ways to help us realize (as far as any of us can) what it must be like to be hungry or sick, to feel unwanted and useless, and to be powerless to alter your situation. Yet in most countries the value of aid from overseas is still less than 7 per cent of the value of exports, so that small changes in the export market can be sufficient to wipe out all the effect of aid.[25] Neither nationally nor internationally has it yet proved possible to translate a widespread concern for the poor into a real 'empowering of the powerless'. One reason is that low export prices paid to the producers of raw materials (which are invariably developing countries) naturally mean low import prices for the manufacturing (developed) coun-tries. Moreover, says Charles Elliott, 'the rich countries fix the price of their exports in relation to the cost of production – so that we carefully build in a certain standard of living to the costs of whatever we export – while we deny that opportunity to the producers of tea or coffee or cocoa or cotton and insist that they price their products at a price that will "clear the market".'[26] It is difficult to resist the conclusion that the rich still exploit the poor. Of course, we must not take refuge in utopian idealism. The total removal of poverty may be only a dream, while the fact remains that 'the poor will always be with you in the land'. But we must complete the quotation: 'and for that reason I command you to be open-handed with your contrymen, both poor and distressed, in your own land.'[27]

Some may seize on the final words, 'in your own land', as an escape hatch from the obligations on us all as human beings. But we do in fact live in one land, one world, with the whole human race as our family, in spite of the resurgent nationalism in many of the European countries which are suffering from recession. Our economies and our security are interlinked, and all talk of national self-sufficiency or indeed national sovereignty, has to reckon with the ever more complex network of obligations and dependencies which no nation can opt out of, however large it may be. The religious traditions of the world – at least where there has been belief in one God – have always preserved this instinct for the brotherhood of common humanity even in their most defensive moments. Their concepts of religious community, whether the people of God, the church, the *Umma* of Islam or the *Khalsa* of the Sikhs, have always been broader than the merely territorial idea of the modern nation-state and have often challenged the narrowness of the latter. At the same time, whatever special role they have seen for themselves, all these groups of believers have clung to the understanding of all human beings without exception as God's children or his cherished servants.

What happens, however, when those who hold the reins of power, even if they profess religious faith, permit or actually initiate the exploitation of the weak, the aged and the poor? What religious resources are there for the ending of tyranny in all its forms? Religious traditions of course have not been slow to identify human perversity in this public and corporate form, and religious literature abounds in the prophetic denunciation of tyranny. But it may well be objected that to ask what religious resources there are for the ending of tyranny is to approach the question the wrong way round. Indeed the prophetic witness claims to analyse and denounce tyranny in the name of a far higher authority, in the name of God. Most of the individual tyrants of history have been unimpressed with the warning of heavenly vengeance in itself, but few can remain entirely unmoved by the erosion of moral authority from their regime. This is particularly so in the modern world, where every government likes to preserve at least the appearance of popular support and fair and honest dealing. The problem for prophetic witness, whether it takes the form of an opposition party, or of Amnesty International, Poland's Solidarity, the South African Council of Churches or some other non-political agency, is that of maintaining the effectiveness of its criticism without being identified as a dangerous threat to society itself. Many unjust governments have been able to remain in power because their critics had to concede that all the likely alternatives were worse.

Thus all right-wing governments are able to cling to power by portraying their opponents as Communists, and Marxist governments by branding theirs as Fascists and imperialists. The only way forward then is either to seize power by all available means, with the real likelihood of replacing one tyranny by another, or to establish by every possible method the purely moral character of your criticism. By 'purely moral' I mean not only devoid of self-interest, but actually keeping firmly in mind the best interests of the wronging, as well as the wronged party. The 'purely moral' critic is able to say with genuine conviction, 'I am fundamentally *for* you as a human being, but. . .' The second quality is much rarer than the first.

The first quality – criticism devoid of self-interest – may be illustrated by the magnificent defiance of the engineer Bobynin in Solzhenitsyn's novel *The First Circle*. Bobynin, and other specially skilled political prisoners, are taken one by one at night to be interviewed by Abakumov, the secret police chief, to report progress on a particular scientific project for Stalin. Abakumov, inwardly nervous about the delay in the project, tries to intimidate Bobynin, who has shown him no respect whatever, although Abakumov 'has the power to imprison half the world'.

– Listen, don't go too far just because I choose to be polite to you. . .

– If you were rude to me I wouldn't talk to you at all. You can shout at your colonels and your generals as much as you like because they've got plenty to lose. . . I own nothing in the world except a handkerchief. . . You took my freedom away a long time ago and you can't give it back to me because you haven't got it yourself. I'm forty-two years old. You gave me twenty-five years. I've done hard labour, I know what it is to have a number instead of a name, to be handcuffed, to be guarded by dogs, to work in a punitive brigade – what more can you do to me? Take me off this special project? You'd be the loser. . . You only have power over people so long as you don't take *everything* away from them. But when you've robbed a man of *everything* he's no longer in your power – he's free again.[28]

Bobynin is powerless, but his very powerlessness gives him great moral authority when he defies Stalin's henchman, and paradoxically great freedom. No one can pretend that he poses anything but a moral threat. But because Bobynin preserves his hatred for Abakumov and everything Abakumov stands for, there is still something missing, something which adds genuine power – spiritual power – to a person's life, because it refuses to hate, refuses to exploit in return for exploitation, but turns instead to a profound pity. 'How could I hate,' wrote John Perkins, black liberation teacher of the Voice of Calvary community in Mississippi, when he was in jail:

How could I hate where there was so much to pity. . . The realization kept pressing on my mind that these men (patrolmen and white thugs) were infected, hopelessly sick, possessed by something which caused their faces to lose that ingredient that made normal features look human, but when missing left faces that could only be described in terms of the animal. . . I saw how my bitterness could destroy me. . . As I lay in bed and thought about God's forgiveness and what it meant to me I began to apply his forgiveness to the faces of the men who had beaten me and to other white people. . . Maybe what frees blacks, frees whites too.[29]

This is the power of the powerless, which Jürgen Moltmann calls 'the name of God, the true God'.[30] The power, the ability, the skill, the talent to think and decide and choose and invent, which God built into his creation, has become hideously distorted. Millions have no power, while the power of others has turned to madness. We are all lost, except for the signs among people like John Perkins of a power at work which is a power of protest and pity mingled. Neither protest, the prophetic voice, however courageous, nor pity, the caring heart, however profound, can by themselves meet our situation.

We need both protest and pity. But that calls for moral and spiritual resources of a very high order. How will we call upon the warring factions of the world's nations to offer one another both protest and pity? In Northern Ireland, in Cyprus, in Lebanon, in Israel, in the Indian Punjab? In Central America? John Perkins began to change when he saw that the brutality of his oppressors diminished them more than it did him. Then he was able to offer them the reconciling gift of pity, as well as the power of protest. But that was at the end of a hard road. Too often religious people, themselves secure from oppression, have taken the easy road of offering pity for the poor and the oppressed when they should have been protesting on their behalf. This has begun to change, but now pity is sometimes forgotten altogether.

Christians believe that in Jesus 'Mercy and truth are met together; righteousness and peace have kissed each other.'[31] In him protest and pity are perfectly balanced, so that in him we see the power of God at work to bring power to the powerless, restoring people to what they were meant to be, people who resemble God because they were made in his image.

Looking Back and Looking Forward

Forty years on from the end of World War II it is understandable that we should take stock of ourselves with some apprehension. Perhaps the most enduring result of the creation of nuclear weapons will not be that they ended the war with Japan, or the dubious claim that they have 'kept the peace' for forty years, but that they have made a massive contribution to a general loss of confidence in the Western culture and way of life. Whenever we attempt to look forward and plan for the future we are faced with the horrifying possibility of nuclear devastation, which could end human existence as we know it. With the previous horrors of the twentieth century in mind there is no reason for confidence that it could never happen.

Since this bleak possibility has arisen within cultures profoundly influenced by Christianity many have turned away from the historic traditions of Christian faith to search for other sources of religious and philosophical insight. There is a burgeoning interest in the religions of the world, and even among those sympathetic to Christian faith a reluctance to commit oneself to the community and institution of the church as an active member. There is no lack of interest in religion, but, at least in Britain, a very strong inclination to pick and choose what one finds attractive about each one. As exotic fruit and vegetables appear in our supermarkets, and taste buds adapt to strange flavours with growing delight, so the vocabulary and customs of the East begin to become familiar to many. And many assume that you select your religion or your philosophy as you shop in the supermarket – as fancy dictates, and as your resources allow.

Unlike the supermarket, however, the religions and philosophies newly imported bring their own criticism of Western history and culture. English-speaking people have been handicapped in recent decades in that they have not generally been compelled to use another language in addition to their mother tongue. Consequently they miss the experience common to millions in the world, of dealing with more than one set of concepts, vocabulary and thought-forms. A Latvian friend told me once how he enjoyed speaking English because there were things he said and thought in English which had no equivalent in his native tongue. The reverse must also have been true. Certainly those of us who lived in Pakistan as expatriates found ourselves adopting Urdu words and expressions into English not merely from habit, but because there was often no English equivalent to them. But where English-speaking people have not had the advantage of this experience they have missed the 'other dimension', the different perspective that another language can bring.

That different perspective always carries with it a measure of criticism, implicit or explicit, of our own ways. Some people feel threatened by criticism, and resent the implication of superiority. I believe that our critics are our friends, saying to us things which our friends are slow to say, if they say them at all. Our critics blow away the mould of complacency and the rust of inertia and hypocrisy on our lives, and force us to face their unpalatable features. This is no less true when we think of the lives of whole communities as of individuals. Listening to Muslims and Jews and others speaking about the history of the Christian churches as they have experienced it, or the way of life that has developed in the West, with its Christian roots, I find myself glad to be able to acknowledge their corporate experience, and the validity of their insights. At the same time I feel no need to betray my own. For what they are telling me is – once again – how little we have lived up to the calling we were given. If I am tempted to argue particular points with them, it is not to deny the general truth that they are putting forward – the truth that no period of history shows unmistakable signs of the proof of Christianity (or any other religion or philosophy).

'We are offered, I believe, a gospel which not only overcomes gloom but also promises glory. But this offer is to be found not where we are confident and at ease but where we are contradicted and at a loss.'[1] Christians claim their faith compels them to a deeper realism about human sin and inadequacy than other faiths, and at the same time that it was in the midst of human evil – personal, religious and political – that the good news of God's liberation of the world in Christ was found. Subsequently Christians indeed became 'confident and at ease' with the way of life they had evolved, at least in the West, and forgot that deeper realism at the heart of their faith. At that point, I believe, many things went wrong. Now we have the opportunity, in an open pluralistic society, to hear the critics of our inherited culture and what God is saying to us through them.

In no way need this mean a denial of the Christian gospel, which after all begins with repentance and continues with forgiveness. Nor need we feel that the integrity of the church is threatened. If the church is a 'society of the unlike' Western Christians have much to learn from fellow-Christians of other cultures, who can help us to learn, unlearn and re-learn as God teaches us through those of other faiths. We do not have a blueprint, nor do we glimpse a Utopia for the society that is to be in our countries, but we bring repentance, compassion and hope in the name of Christ into all the relationships that will be ours in it.

Notes

Introduction

1 Matthew 13:29–30

Chapter One Education

1 *Muslim Education*. This quarterly journal published by the King Abdulaziz University, Jeddah, Saudi Arabia, currently prints this statement inside the front cover of each issue.

2 S. N. Al-Attas, *Aims and Objectives of Islamic Education*, King Abdulaziz University, Jeddah, 1979, p. 1.

3 Ivan Illich, *Deschooling Society*, Penguin Books, 1971, pp. 9, 20

4 Robert Jeffcoate, *Positive Image. Towards a Multi-racial Curriculum*. Writers and Readers Publishing Co-operative, London, 1979, p. 36. Much else in this chaper I owe to this book

5 Robert Jeffcoate *Positive Image*, p. 36

6 Preiswerk (editor), *The Slant of the Pen. Racism in Children's Books*, World Council of Churches, Geneva, 1981, pp. 38, 39

7 Preiswerk, *The Slant of the Pen*, p. 123

8 *The Observer*, 4 March 1984, article by Prof. John Kenyon

9 CMND 6869, Her Majesty's Stationery Office, 1977 (quoted in *Schools and Multi-Cultural Education*, a paper from the Church of England Board of Education, 1984)

10 Quoted in *Linguistic Minorities in England* (a report from the Linguistic Minorities Project for the Department of Education and Science), University of London, 1983, p. 23

11 *Linguistic Minorities in England*, 1983, p. 23

12 W. Owen Cole (editor), *World Faiths in Education*, Allen and Unwin, 1978, p. 15

13 Edward Hulmes, *Commitment and Neutrality in Religious Education*, Geoffrey Chapman, 1979, p. 29

14 W. Owen Cole, *Religion in the Multi-Faith School*, Hulton, 1983, p. 11

15 McDermott and Ahsan, *The Muslim Guide*, The Islamic Foundation, Leicester, 1980, pp. 46, 72f.

16 *Muslim Education*, see above

17 For example by Lord Scarman, in a speech to education officers in January 1982

18 *The Guardian*, 13 April 1983 (quoted in *Schools and Multi-Cultural Education*, 1984)

19 *A Future in Partnership*, National Society (Church of England) for Promoting Religious Education, London, 1984, p. 88

20 *The Muslim Guide*, p. 51, 52

21 *A Future in Partnership*, p. 90

22 *A Future in Partnership*, p. 91

Chapter Two Blessing and Refuge

1 Matthew 18:26

2 Revelation 19:10; 22:8

3 R. S. Thomas, 'The Absence' from *Later Poems 1972–1982*, Macmillan, 1983, p. 123

4 R. S. Thomas, *Later Poems 1972–1982*, p. 112

5 Lisbeth Sachs, *Evil Eye or Bacteria. Turkish Migrant Women and Swedish Health Care*, Stockholm 1983, p. 95

6 Lisbeth Sachs, *Evil Eye or Bacteria*, p. 157

7 M. M. Pickthall (translator), *The Meaning of the Glorious Koran*, sura 113

8 Quoted in Kenneth Cragg, *The Event of the Qur'an*, Allen and Unwin, 1971, p. 82

9 Ezekiel 3:1–3

10 Revelation 10:9–11

11 Mary Douglas, *Purity and Danger. An Analysis of Concepts of Pollution and Taboo*, Routledge and Kegan Paul, 1966, p. 90

12 Lesslie Newbigin, *The Other Side of 1984. Questions for the Churches*. World Council of Churches, 1983, p. 9

13 Lisbeth Sachs, *Evil Eye or Bacteria*, p. 77f.

14 Mary Douglas, *Purity and Danger*, p. 136

15 Genesis 4:6–7

16 Mary Douglas, *Purity and Danger*, pp. 110, 111. See also Norman Cohn, *Europe's Inner Demons*, Paladin, 1975; and Christina Larner, *Enemies of God. The Witch-*

Hunt in Scotland, Blackwell, 1983

17 Bede, *A History of the English Church and People*, Penguin edition, 1955, p. 153 (Book 3, chapter 9)

18 Matthew 12:26–27

19 Matthew 12:33

20 John Berger and Jean Mohr, *A Fortunate Man. The Story of a Country Doctor*, Penguin Books, 1967, p. 60f.

21 H. R. Ellis Davidson, *Gods and Myths of Northern Europe*, Penguin Books, 1964, p. 144

22 Brian Bates, *The Way of Wyrd, Tales of an Anglo-Saxon Sorcerer*, Century Publishing, 1983

23 Brian Bates, *The Way of Wyrd*, p. 74

24 Brian Bates, *The Way of Wyrd*, p. 88

25 H. R. Ellis Davidson, *Gods and Myths of Northern Europe*, p. 50

26 Alan D. Gilbert, *The Making of Post-Christian Britain*, Longman, 1980, p. 153

27 Acts of the Apostles 17:26–28

28 *Can We Pray Together? Guidelines on Worship in a Multi-Faith Society*, British Council of Churches, 1983, p. 4. A full discussion of the issue is found here.

29 Some excellent material is contained in John Bailey's *Themework*. Assembly Material for Junior, Middle and Lower Secondary Schools, Stainer and Bell, 1981

30 *The Mathnawi*, quoted by R. A. Nicholson in *The Mystics of Islam* (first published 1914) Routledge and Kegan Paul, 1975, p. 113

Chapter Three   Food

1 Alan Unterman, *Jews. Their Religious Beliefs and Practices*, Routledge and Kegan Paul, 1981, p. 201

2 Mark 7:18–19

3 Lionel Blue and June Rose, *A Taste of Heaven, Adventures in Food and Faith*, Darton, Longman and Todd, 1977, p. 84

4 Deuteronomy 14:21

5 Lionel Blue and June Rose, *A Taste of Heaven*, p. 49

6 *Pirke Aboth* III.4

7 Leviticus 7:25

8 Genesis 32:33

9 Leviticus 7:26

10 Qur'an 2:187

11 Qur'an 2:185

12 Qur'an 2:173

13 Qur'an 6:147

14 Qur'an 2:219

15 *The Muslim Guide*. For teachers, employers, community workers and social administrators in Britain, published by the Islamic Foundation, Leicester, 1980, p. 36f.

16 David G. Bowen (editor), *Hinduism in England*, Bradford College, 1981, pp. 86, 64

17 Cole and Sambhi, *The Sikhs. Their Religious Beliefs and Practices*, Routledge and Kegan Paul, 1978, p. 124

18 Cole and Sambhi, *The Sikhs*, p. 141

19 Cole and Sambhi, *The Sikhs*, p. 33

20 John Carden, *Empty Shoes. A Way in to Pakistan*, Highway Press, 1971, p. 15

21 Hebrews 13:2

22 Genesis 18

23 Lionel Blue and June Rose, *A Taste of Heaven*, p. 86

24 Mark 7:19

Chapter Four   Sex and Gender

1 Patricia Jeffery, *Frogs in a Well: Indian Women in Purdah*, Zed Press, 1979, p.12

2 *The Muslim Guide*, The Islamic Foundation, Leicester, 1980, p. 81

3 *The Muslim Guide*, p. 83ff.

4 Nawal El Saadawi, *The Hidden Face of Eve: Women in the Arab World*, Zed Press, 1980, pp. 24, 23

5 Nawal El Saadawi, *The Hidden Face of Eve*, p. 211

6 Wendy Doniger O'Flaherty, *Siva: The Erotic Ascetic*, Oxford University Press, 1981 edition, p. 1

7 R. C. Zaehner, *Hinduism*, Oxford University Press, 1962, p. 113, quoted in O'Flaherty, *Siva*, p. 5

8 Details taken from O'Flaherty, *Siva*, p. 30ff.

9 Nirad Chaudhuri, *Hinduism: A Religion to Live By*, Chatto and Windus, 1979, pp. 9–10

10 Nirad Chaudhuri, *Hinduism*, p. 270

11 Genesis 1:27
12 Genesis 1:28
13 Genesis 3:16
14 Galatians 3:28
15 2 Corinthians 5:17

Chapter Five   Marriage and Family

1 Patricia Jeffery, *Frogs in a Well: Indian Women in Purdah*, Zed Press, 1979 p. 10f.
2 Patricia Jeffery, *Frogs in a Well*, p. 56
3 Amrit Wilson, *Finding a Voice: Asian Women in Britain*, Virago, 1978, p. 114
4 Rabbi Dow Marmur, from a pamphlet entitled *Intermarriage*, Reform Synagogues of Great Britain, London
5 Rabbi Dow Marmur, *Beyond Survival*, Darton, Longman and Todd, 1982
6 Christopher Lamb, *Mixed Faith Marriage. A Case for Care*, British Council of Churches, 1982
7 Quoted in Cole and Sambhi, *The Sikhs: Their Religious Beliefs and Practices*, Routledge and Kegan Paul, 1978, p. 116
8 1 Corinthians 7:12–16
9 2 Corinthians 6:14
10 *The Guardian*, 4 September 1982

Chapter Six   Health and handicap

1 N. W. Clerk, *A Grief Observed*, Faber and Faber, 1961, pp. 12, 13
2 Isaiah 53:3
3 William Shakespeare, *Antony and Cleopatra*, Act 2, scene 5
4 Luke 9:1
5 R. H. Hooker, *Voices of Varanasi*, Church Missionary Society, 1979, pp. 67, 68
6 Peter Speck, *Loss and Grief in Medicine*, Baillière Tindall, 1978, pp. 24f, 144
7 M. A. H. Melinsky (editor), *Religion and Medicine. A Discussion*, SCM Press, 1970, p. 114
8 C. Saunders (editor), *Hospice: The Living Idea*, Edward Arnold, 1981, p. 93
9 C. Saunders, *Hospice: The Living Idea*, p. 4
10 C. S. Song, *Third-Eye Theology*, Lutterworth Press, 1980, pp. 67, 68
11 N. W. Clerk, *A Grief Observed*, p. 27f.
12 Revelation 5:6
13 Revelation 1:17,18
14 Revelation 21:3,4
15 J. V. Taylor, *The Primal Vision*, SCM Press, 1963, p. 70f.
16 *Religions and Cultures. A guide to patients' beliefs and customs for health service staff*, 1978. Available from Lothian Community Relations Council, 12A Forth Street, Edinburgh EH1 3LH
17 Genesis 2:18
18 1 Corinthians 12:26

Chapter Seven   Morality and Law

1 *The Times*, 24 July 1981
2 John Habgood, *Church and Nation in a Secular Age*, Darton, Longman and Todd, 1983, pp. 60, 61
3 *The Guardian*, 7 February 1984
4 *Report on Homosexual Offences and Prostitution* 1957, paragraph 61
5 Exodus 21:18–19
6 Exodus 20:12
7 Lionel Blue, *To Heaven with Scribes and Pharisees. The Jewish Path to God*, Darton, Longman and Todd, 1975, p. 20f.
8 See, for example, the section on Blood-money in Imam Malik, *Al-Muwatta*, Diwan Press, 1982, pp. 407–17
9 *Encyclopaedia of Islam*, new edition, Brill, 1961, article 'Hadd'
10 Deuteronomy 19:16–21
11 Matthew 6:14–15
12 Matthew 18:21–35
13 Luke 23:34
14 Acts of the Apostles 7:60
15 1 Peter 2:23
16 Reinhold Niebuhr, *Moral Man and Immoral Society*, first British edition 1963, SCM Press, p. 1 (originally published in 1932)
17 *Encyclopaedia of Religion and Ethics*, article 'Confession'

18 R. Panikkar, *The Vedic Experience*, Darton, Longman and Todd, 1977, p. 491

19 R. Panikkar, *The Vedic Experience*, p. 492

20 V. S. Naipaul, *India; A Wounded Civilization*, Deutsch, 1977, p. 107, quoting U. R. Anantamurti's *Samskara*

21 *The Guardian*, 12 July 1982

22 Mark 2:27

23 Quoted in John Habgood, *Church and Nation in a Secular Age*, p. 62f

24 Reinhold Niebuhr, *Moral Man and Immoral Society*, p. 277

25 John Habgood, *Church and Nation in a Secular Age*, p. 64

Chapter Eight   Work and Achievement

1 Quoted in Lionel Blue, *To Heaven with Scribes and Pharisees. The Jewish Path to God*, Darton, Longman and Todd, 1975, p. 102

2 David Bleakley, *Work: The Shadow and the Substance*, SCM Press, 1983, p. 92

3 David Bleakley, *In Place of Work. . . The Sufficient Society*, SCM Press, 1981, p. 40f.

4 For much of the basic data of this chapter I am indebted to David Bleakley's two books cited above.

5 Lionel Blue, *To Heaven with Scribes and Pharisees*, p. 18f

6 See, for example, Rabbi Tarphon: 'If thou hast studied much Torah, much reward will be given thee.' *Pirke Aboth* 2:21

7 *Pirke Aboth* 2:19

8 Lionel Blue, *To Heaven with Scribes and Pharisees*, pp. 24, 25

9 David Bleakley, *Work: The Shadow and the Substance*, p. 77

10 R. H. Tawney, *Religion and the Rise of Capitalism*, (first published 1922), Penguin edition 1980, p. 119

11 Max Weber, *The Protestant Ethic*, (first German edition 1905). English edition 1930, p. 175

12 Max Weber, *The Protestant Ethic*, p. 177

13 Micah 4:4

14 David Bleakley, *Work: The Shadow and the Substance*, p. 80

15 *The Observer*, 28 March 1982

16 *The Times*, 9 January 1982

17 *The Observer*, 28 March 1982

18 Eugen Herrigel, *Zen in the Art of Archery*, Routledge and Kegan Paul, 1972, p. 96

19 Hirohide Ogawa, *Enlightenment through the Art of Basketball*, Oleander Press, 1979. This book has no pagination, presumably to convey the message that each page is saying the same thing

20 Hirohide Ogawa, *Enlightenment through the Art of Basketball*

21 David Bleakley, *In Place of Work*, p. 95

22 Dow Marmur, *Beyond Survival. Reflections on the Future of Judaism*, Darton, Longman and Todd, 1982, p. 135

23 Hirohide Ogawa, *Enlightenment through the Art of Basketball*

24 Winston L. King, 'A Christian and a Japanese-Buddhist Work-Ethic Compared' in *Religion*, 1981, volume 11, pp. 207-26

25 Winston L. King, 'A Christian and a Japanese-Buddhist Work-Ethic Compared'

26 *Gita* 2:47

27 M. K. Gandhi, *M. K. Gandhi Interprets the Bhagvadgita*, Orient Paperbacks, New Delhi, India, p. 148. (These addresses were given in 1926.)

28 Matthew 25:31-46

29 Matthew 6:3

30 *Gita* 2:47

31 Nirad Chaudhuri, *Hinduism. A Religion to Live By*, Chatto and Windus, 1979, p. 267

32 See Dow Marmur, *Beyond Survival*, p. 130ff.

33 H. Bettenson (editor), *Documents of the Christian Church*, Oxford University Press, 1943, p. 171

34 Matthew 20:1-16

35 Matthew 20:20-28

36 Luke 17:10

37 David Bleakley, *In Place of Work*, p. 82

38 1 Corinthians 15:58

Chapter Nine   Freedom and Truth in the Media

1 Glasgow University Media Group, *Bad News*, Routledge and Kegan Paul, 1976, p. 2
2 *New Internationalist*, September 1982, p. 25
3 *New Internationalist*, September 1982, pp. 26–28
4 *Bad News*, p. 12
5 Glasgow University Media Group, *More Bad News*, Routledge and Kegan Paul, 1980, p. vii
6 Altaf Gauhar, *South-South Strategy*, Third World Foundation, 1983, p. 78
7 Altaf Gauhar, *South-South Strategy*, pp. 88, 89
8 *New Internationalist*, September 1982, p. 28
9 Commonwealth Secretariat, *The North-South Dialogue*, London, 1982
10 *Arabia, The Islamic World Review*, October 1981, p. 36
11 For this and following quotations, see Altaf Gauhar, *South-South Strategy*, pp. 74–77
12 H. B. Dehqani-Tafti, *The Hard Awakening*, SPCK, 1981, p. 35
13 In three books entitled *Orientalism* (1979), *The Question of Palestine*, (1979) and *Covering Islam* (1981)
14 Edward Said, *Covering Islam: How the Media and the Experts Determine How We See the Rest of the World*, New York, 1981, p. ix
15 Edward Said, *Covering Islam*, p. xvii
16 Edward Said, *Covering Islam*, p. xv
17 Edward Said, *Covering Islam*, p. 26
18 Edward Said, *Covering Islam*, p. 79 and other places
19 Edward Said, *Covering Islam*, p. 23
20 Marius Baar, *The Unholy War: Oil, Islam and Armageddon*, Henry E. Walter, 1980
21 Ishak Ibraham, *Black Gold and Holy War: The religious secret behind the petrodollar*, Marshalls, 1982
22 *Journal of Palestine Studies*, XI.1, Autumn 1981, p. 164
23 *The Times*, 20 July 1981
24 Sellar and Yeatman, *1066 and All That*, Methuen, 1959, p. v (first published 1930)
25 See Matthew 5:28
26 Acts of the Apostles 14:17
27 Matthew 4:4, quoting Deuteronomy 8:3
28 See Christopher Lamb, *Jesus Through Other Eyes: Christology in Multi-Faith Context*, Latimer House, Oxford, 1982, p. 19
29 2 Corinthians 5:19

Chapter Ten   Wealth and Power

1 Matthew 5:5
2 Mohammed Ayoob, *The Politics of Islamic Reassertion*, Croom Helm, 1981, pp. 288, 289
3 Mohammed Ayoob, *The Politics of Islamic Reassertion*, p. 289
4 Clifford Geertz, *Islam Observed*, quoted in Mohammed Ayoob, *The Politics of Islamic Reassertion*, p. 5
5 See, for example, the thesis of Alastair Kee in *Constantine Versus Christ* (SCM Press, 1982) that Constantine was not converted to genuine Christianity. Rather his imperial ideology came to be called 'Christianity'. The real thing has suffered this misrepresentation ever since in Europe.
6 See, for example, V. S. Naipaul, *Among the Believers*, Penguin edition, 1982, especially p. 98f.
7 Mark 1:15
8 Quoted in *Resurgence* magazine, September–October 1974. I owe this reference to Dr Edie Friedman
9 Quoted in *Resurgence*, September–October 1974
10 Seyyed Hossein Nasr, *Islam and the Plight of Modern Man*, Longman, 1975, pp. 4, 13
11 Dietrich Bonhoeffer, *Letters and Papers from Prison*, Fontana edition, 1959, p. 106f.
12 Dietrich Bonhoeffer, *Letters and Papers from Prison*, p. 109
13 The Qur'an, sura 96:6–8. Translation by A. J. Arberry, *The Koran Interpreted*, Oxford University Press, 1964, p. 651
14 Kenneth Cragg, *The Mind of the Qur'an*, Allen and Unwin, 1973, p. 136
15 Sura 93. A. J. Arberry, *The Koran*

Interpreted, p. 648
16 James 1:27
17 The title of a book by David
    Sheppard, Bishop of Liverpool,
    published by Hodder and
    Stoughton, 1983
18 Amos 5:23,24
19 Matthew 25:31–46
20 David Sheppard, *Bias to the Poor*,
    p. 17
21 David Sheppard, *Bias to the Poor*,
    p. 11
22 Leviticus 25:35,36
23 Charles Elliott, *Power, Salvation and
    Suffering. The 1983 CMS Annual
    Sermon*, Church Missionary Society,
    London, 1983, pp. 2,4
24 David Sheppard, *Bias to the Poor*,
    p. 69
25 Charles Elliott, *Power, Salvation and
    Suffering*, p. 4
26 Charles Elliott, *Power Salvation and
    Suffering*, p. 4
27 Deuteronomy 15:11
28 Alexander Solzhenitsyn, *The First
    Circle*, English translation Harvill
    Press, 1968, p. 85
29 Quoted in the *CMS Newsletter*, no.
    458, January 1984
30 Jürgen Moltmann, *The Power of the
    Powerless*, SCM Press, 1983, p. x
31 Psalm 85:10

Postscript
 1 David Jenkins, *The Contradiction of
    Christianity*, SCM Press, 1976, p. 5

Readers of this book may require more information than is available here, or guidance on how to make contact with people from minority communities. **Christopher Lamb** is employed by two Anglican societies for just this purpose, and can be contacted at: 44 Weoley Park Road, Selly Oak, Birmingham B29 6RB